Science Fair Projects

WITH EVERYDAY STUFF

★ PRIZE-WINNING Science Fair Projects ★

Science Fair Projects

WITH EVERYDAY STUFF

Salvatore
Tocci

E **Enslow Publishing**
101 W. 23rd Street
Suite 240
New York, NY 10011
USA
enslow.com

Published in 2016 by Enslow Publishing, LLC
101 W. 23rd Street, Suite 240, New York, NY 10011

Cataloging-in-Publication Data
Tocci, Salvatore.
  Science fair projects with everyday stuff / by Salvatore Tocci.
     p. cm. — (Prize-winning science fair projects)
  Includes bibliographical references and index.
  ISBN 978-0-7660-7020-2 (library binding)
  1. Science projects — Juvenile literature. I. Tocci, Salvatore. II. Title.
  Q164.T36 2016
  507'.8—d23

Printed in the United States of America

To Our Readers: We have done our best to make sure all Web site addresses in this book were active and appropriate when we went to press. However, the author and the publisher have no control over and assume no liability for the material available on those Web sites or on any Web sites they may link to. Any comments or suggestions can be sent by e-mail to customerservice@enslow.com.

Portions of this book originally appeared in the book *Science Fair Success Using Household Products.*

Illustration Credits: Modification of original art by Accurate Art, Inc; c/o George Barile; Enslow Publishing, LLC, pp. 61, 88, 90, 110; Gary Koelhoffer, Crooked Grin Design, pp. 21, 24, 33, 44, 50, 52, 68, 69, 73, 102, 106, 108; Stephen F. Delisle, pp. 26, 40, 76, 104, 116.

Photo Credits: Africa Studio/Shutterstock.com, p. 3 (starch in spoon); AlenKadr/Shutterstock.com, p. 3 (toothbrush); Andrei Kuzmik/Shutterstock.com, p. 3 (toothpaste); Anest/Shutterstock.com, p. 3 (green dishwashing liquid); deniss09/Shutterstock.com, p. 3 (honey); design56/Shutterstock.com, p. 3 (lemon juice); hadkhanong/Shutterstock.com, p. 3 (liquid soap); KIM NGUYEN/Shutterstock.com, p. 3 (pink dishwashing liquid); Ohn Mar/Shutterstock.com (science background throughout book); Studio KIWI/Shutterstock.com, p. 3 (bottle of suntan cream); TAGSTOCK1/Shutterstock.com, p. 80; TrotzOlga/Shutterstock.com, p. 3 (rubber gloves); Tyler Olsen/Shutterstock.com, p. 18.

Cover Credits: Africa Studio/Shutterstock.com (starch in spoon); AlenKadr/Shutterstock.com (toothbrush); Andrei Kuzmik/Shutterstock.com (toothpaste); Anest/Shutterstock.com (green dishwashing liquid); deniss09/Shutterstock.com (honey); design56/Shutterstock.com (lemon juice); hadkhanong/Shutterstock.com (liquid soap); KIM NGUYEN/Shutterstock.com (pink dishwashing liquid); Ohn Mar/Shutterstock.com (science background); Studio KIWI/Shutterstock.com (bottle of suntan cream); TrotzOlga/Shutterstock.com (rubber gloves).

CONTENTS

periments with a ⭐ symbol feature Project Ideas and Further Investigations.

Experiments with a ★ symbol feature Project Ideas and Further Investigation

INTRODUCTION

Science may be your favorite subject in school. Like many students, perhaps the reason you like science is because you like to carry out experiments. Most students find it fun to mix chemicals, pour solutions, or work with scientific equipment. They are often surprised by what they see. The chemicals may turn a different color, the solutions may start to bubble, or a microscope may reveal a rather unusual-looking creature living in a drop of pond water.

If you like to do experiments, then you have come to the right place. The experiments in this book are designed to use products that you can easily find at home, including toothpaste, aspirin, and dishwashing detergent. Each experiment in this book is designed to teach you something about the science behind these products. For example, you will learn why water alone cannot remove the grease from your hands or dirty clothes. To get really clean, you need soap or detergent.

Most of the experiments in this book will also make you a better educated consumer. For example, you may discover which toothpaste cleans your teeth best, which aspirin is least likely to upset your stomach, or which detergent gets the dirt out of your clothes best. As a result, your next purchase of a household product may be based on what you learn from this book and not because of what you hear or read in an advertisement. But most of all, you should find the experiments in this book fun to do.

Benefits of Doing Experiments

When you perform an experiment, you actually get to do science rather than simply read or hear about it. Experiments allow you to be an active participant in your learning process. Performing experiments can be a more interesting way to learn, compared to reading about science from a book or listening to someone explain it. This is not to say that reading and listening are not important. But there are times when an experiment is a more effective way to learn and understand. Doing an experiment can also be more challenging and force you to think. In effect, performing an experiment allows you to play the role of detective. You must observe closely and arrive at some answer to explain what happened.

Experiments often allow you to be creative. True, the directions as to what to do in an experiment in school are always provided. But there is nothing preventing you from adding your own ideas. For example, the directions may call for gently heating a solution to see what happens. But you may decide to see what happens if you slowly cool the same solution. Perhaps you will observe something that was totally unexpected. There is one very important caution if you decide to investigate something on your own: Be sure to check with your science teacher or an adult before you do the experiment. Have them review your plan before you start. In that way, you will not be putting yourself or anyone else in danger.

The reason you do an experiment is to answer a question or solve a problem. But experiments often lead to more questions. For example, this book describes an experiment designed to show how an antacid works in reducing excess stomach acid. After you finish the experiment, you may want to check to see if other antacid products work as well or even better. You can also investigate whether antacids are more effective when their temperature is close to body temperature rather than to room temperature. In effect, the results of one experiment can easily lead you to start thinking about doing another experiment.

Almost none of the experiments that you do in school will produce any surprises. That is because the experiment has been designed so that you are sure to learn something about the topic you are studying. But be aware that not all experiments are like this. Scientists often observe things that they did not expect to see in their experiments. This is another reason that experiments are fun to do. In many cases, these unexpected observations have led to some valuable findings. Penicillin and nylon are just two of the many discoveries that were made unexpectedly by scientists. The possibility of an unusual outcome adds to the excitement of carrying out an experiment, so be sure to observe closely and note everything that happens in an experiment. You can always check with your science teacher if you think that something unexpected did happen.

The Scientific Method

Just like a detective, a scientist does not proceed in a random fashion. Rather, both a detective and scientist carefully plan what they are going to do. They also carry out their work very precisely, hoping to arrive at some answer or solution. The process scientists use in carrying out their work is known as the scientific method. Performing an experiment is often one of the steps that make up the scientific method.

Scientists can choose from a wide variety of steps to use in their work. Table 1 lists some of these steps, or scientific processes. Notice that some of these scientific processes are ones that many people use in their daily lives. For example, observing is something that a farmer, builder, truck driver, and many other people do as part of their job. In fact, any one of the scientific processes listed in Table 1 can be used by anybody. Consider a truck driver who wants to get to a destination sooner. The driver may have reason to believe that a different route will accomplish this goal. In fact, the driver may experiment by trying several different routes. Although the processes listed in Table 1 can be used at times by anyone, these processes are used all the time by scientists. Without them, scientists would not be able to work.

A scientist will choose which steps of the scientific method are needed for a particular experiment or investigation. For example, collecting information in the field may be part of the scientific method used by a scientist who is studying bird migration. On the other hand, this process would not be used by a scientist who is trying to develop a new antibiotic.

Purpose	Process
Collect Information	Observe Conduct field studies Measure Sample Organize data
Hypothesize	Form a hypothesis Predict
Experiment	Conduct a controlled experiment Solve problems Analyze data Evaluate data Communicate
Draw conclusions	Design a model Infer Form a theory

Table 1. The Scientific Method

As you go through this book, you will use many of the scientific processes that are listed in Table 1. The processes you use in each case will make up the scientific method that you follow for that particular experiment. You may find that you use certain processes more often than others. One scientific process that you are certain to use almost every time you do an experiment is recording information.

Keeping Accurate Records

A good scientist keeps thorough and detailed records. This is especially important if the scientist is trying a new procedure or has made an interesting observation. You, too, must keep a complete record of what you do. For each experiment in this book, the purpose of the experiment is given. Also given is a list of what you need and a procedure to follow. But you will not be told what results your experiment will give. In fact, no one—not even your science teacher—will know what the results will be for many of the experiments in this book. That is because it all depends on what you do. For example, if you decide to experiment with aspirin, you have the option of using any brand you wish. No one you know, including your science teacher, has likely tested the aspirin product you choose. Thus, no one will know what the results will be until you have finished your experiment.

To arrive at some conclusion, you will have to examine the information that you collect in your experiments. Information and observations collected in an experiment are known as data. You must record all your data in a notebook that you use solely for the experiments you decide to do. Your data must be neat, organized, and accurate. Only then can you arrive at a valid conclusion based on your data. You will be told what data to record as you proceed through each experiment.

Variables and Controls

Experiments are designed to provide an answer to some question or a solution to some problem. In designing an experiment, a scientist selects something that he or she feels will affect the outcome or results. For example, a scientist may be interested in stopping the growth of certain cells. The scientist may have developed a drug for such a purpose. Obviously, the scientist will expose the cells to the drug and see if they stop growing. The scientist can select how much of the drug to give, the number of doses that are used, the time interval between doses, and so on. But the scientist will usually test only one thing at a time. Thus, the first round of experiments might involve testing to see how much of the drug is needed to stop cell growth.

In designing the experiment, the scientist might expose a group of cells to a certain dosage of the drug, another group of cells to twice the dosage, a third group to three times the dosage, and so on. In each case, the amount of the drug used represents the independent variable. A variable is something that can change during an experiment. An independent variable is one that the investigator is free to change at any time during the course of the experiment.

What happens to the cells exposed to the drug represents the dependent variable. A dependent variable is something that can change depending on what the investigator does. In this experiment, the cells may continue to grow, stop growing, or even grow faster, depending on the dosage used.

In designing the experiment, the scientist will be sure to follow certain procedures. For example, each group will contain the same number of cells. Each group will receive the dosage at the same time and under the same conditions. In other words, the only difference between each group will be how much drug they receive. Each experiment should have only one independent variable. That way the scientist can be sure that if the cells stop growing in one group, the reason can only be the dosage that was used.

The scientist will also be sure to set up a group of cells that will not be exposed to the drug. These cells represent the control group. Cells that are exposed to the drug represent an experimental group. Consider what happens if the cells in an experimental group stop growing, but the cells in the control group continue to grow. In this case, the scientist can conclude that the drug was responsible. In other words, a control group helps a scientist rule out other causes for what happened.

As you carry out any experiment in this book, be sure that you identify the independent variable, dependent variable, experimental group, and control group. If you change an experiment, be sure that each of these is still included in your new design. If you do not, then you will not be able to make a valid conclusion.

Science Projects

You may be looking to do a science project as part of a class assignment. Or your school may be sponsoring a science fair where each student must enter a project. There is also the possibility that you want to do a science project just to learn something and to have some fun. Whatever the reason, be sure to follow the same guidelines that have been provided for doing an experiment. But do not stop there. A project by definition is more involved than an experiment. A project implies that a person has spent more time and effort than is required for carrying out a single experiment.

Most experiments in this book can be the starting point for a science project. For example, you may carry out the experiment that analyzes an aspirin tablet. You can easily expand this experiment into a project by comparing different brands of aspirin. You can also do some research to find out how aspirin works by checking at a library or searching the Internet. You might include information about aspirin substitutes. If you run across a problem, you could contact the company for help or advice. Science fair judges will be impressed if you have shown some initiative. Also be sure to find out how to set up and present your project. You will find some resources on these topics listed in the further reading section of this book.

Safety First

When doing an experiment or carrying out a project, the most important thing to keep in mind is safety. Doing science can be dangerous at times. Many chemicals are poisonous. Many solutions are flammable. Glassware is breakable and can cause injury. Some liquids may splatter and get into your eyes. Other liquids may burn your skin. To avoid an accident, always keep the following safety precautions in mind:

1. Be sure to follow all safety warnings, especially when you are advised to work under the supervision of an adult.
2. When in doubt, first check with your science teacher or another adult.
3. Do not eat or drink in the area where you are experimenting.
4. Always wear safety goggles. You can purchase a pair at a hardware store. Be sure to remove any contact lenses. Chemicals can get between your contact lenses and your eyes and cause

damage. You may also want to wear a lab apron to protect your clothing.

5. Be sure to tie back any loose hair or clothing, especially when working near an open flame.

6. If a chemical spills on your skin, place the area under running water. Be sure to inform an adult immediately.

7. Be sure to wash your hands with soap and water when you are finished with your experiment.

8. Use common sense. The best way to avoid an accident is to prevent it. Never fool around while you are experimenting. Keep your work area clean. Never taste chemicals or touch them with your bare hands.

If you follow these safety rules, your work should proceed smoothly. What's more, you will not lose out on the fun of doing experiments.

Chapter 1

KEEPING YOU CLEAN

Using toothpaste, soap, and shampoo are part of an everyday personal hygiene routine. You and your family most likely have many personal hygiene products use on your skin, teeth, and hair. Keeping clean is one way to prevent germs from entering the body and causing disease. Germs are living things that are so small they can only be seen with a magnifying lens or a microscope. These very tiny living things are known as microorganisms. The prefix *micro* means "very small." An organism is any living thing.

Microorganisms were first seen in the mid-1600s by a Dutchman named Antoni van Leeuwenhoek. During his life, Leeuwenhoek made hundreds of glass lenses to study tiny objects. He also examined a variety of liquids, including saliva, blood, and water collected from different sources such as ponds and wells. Leeuwenhoek became the first person to see and describe the miniature world of microorganisms.

However, Leeuwenhoek had no idea that many of the microorganisms he examined could cause disease. In fact, almost two hundred years would pass before a connection between microorganisms and disease would be discovered. In the 1840s, a

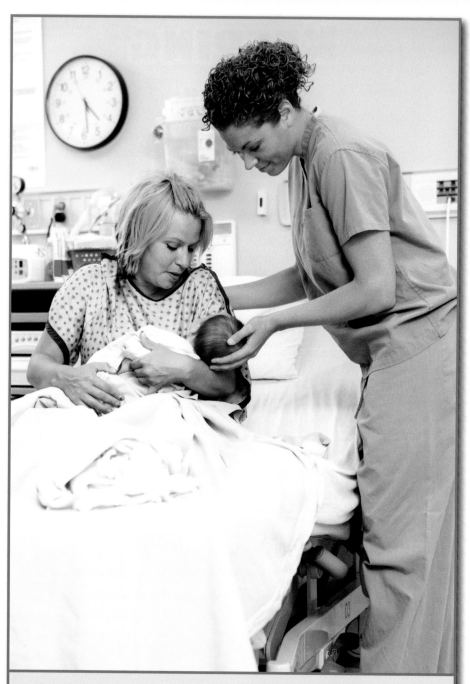

Modern hospitals and maternity wards now use sterile techniques to keep germs from spreading.

Hungarian doctor named Ignaz Semmelweis was working in the maternity ward of a hospital. He was concerned about the number of women who died after giving birth. Semmelweis was shocked to discover that in some cases up to 50 percent of the women died following childbirth.

Semmelweis made an interesting observation. The death rate following childbirth was much higher in the maternity wards where medical students delivered the babies than in those wards where trained women delivered the babies. Semmelweis compared various conditions between the two wards, including bed linens, crowding, ventilation, and the food served. He found them to be the same in both wards. Obviously, none of these conditions could be the cause.

Semmelweis then noticed that the medical students rarely washed their hands before delivering a baby. In many cases, these students had just performed an autopsy. Semmelweis believed that the medical students were spreading a disease on their hands to the women who were having babies. He insisted that the medical students scrub their hands with soap and water before delivering any baby. For the first time, the death rate in the maternity wards staffed by medical students dropped below the death rate in the wards staffed by the trained women.

Unfortunately, the value of Semmelweis' work was not recognized immediately. In fact, his superiors at the hospital ridiculed the requirement that medical students wash their hands before delivering a baby. After years of ridicule and abuse, Semmelweis quit working at the hospital. He died in 1865. The importance of washing with soap to get rid of germs would not be appreciated until several years after his death.

Experiment 1.1
GETTING RID OF GERMS

Washing gets rid of the germs and dirt that become trapped in the oils and grease on your skin. If you just wash with water, no matter how hard you scrub, your skin will never get really clean. Oils and grease cannot mix with water, so water alone cannot get rid of the germs and dirt embedded in them. This is where soap is needed.

Think of soap as a person with outstretched arms. Now imagine a lot of people with outstretched arms, with one hand grabbing on to water and their other hand grabbing on to grease. Now imagine what happens when all these people start to move around very quickly. As the people move about, the water and grease will mix. The same thing happens when you scrub with soap. One "hand" of soap grabs on to water. The other "hand" grabs on to grease. As you scrub, the soap moves around and mixes the water and grease. The harder you scrub, the cleaner you get because rinsing with water can now wash away the germs and dirt that were trapped in the grease. This experiment will examine how well a hand soap gets rid of grease.

Use your finger to cover both sides of two identical teaspoons with a very light coating of vegetable shortening, as shown in

Materials

* 2 teaspoons
* vegetable shortening
* 2 identical small drinking glasses
* measuring cup
* alcohol thermometer
* liquid hand soap
* clock or watch
* optional: several additional brands of liquid hand soap

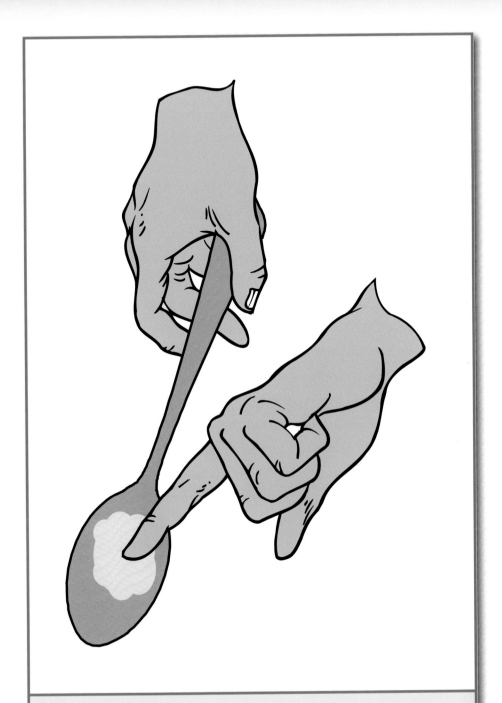

Figure 1. Cover both sides of the bowl of a spoon with a uniform, light coating of vegetable shortening.

Figure 1. Vegetable shortening is a grease. Try your best to apply the same amount of shortening to each spoon. Place each spoon in one of two identical small glasses of warm water. Use a measuring cup to be sure that the level of water in each glass is the same. Use a thermometer to be sure that the temperature of the water in each glass is the same.

Add one drop of liquid hand soap to one of the glasses. Gently stir the spoons in both glasses for two minutes. Remove the spoons. Examine them to compare how much shortening is left on each spoon. The spoon stirred in the glass of water that has no soap added is the control.

Continue adding the liquid soap to the first glass, one drop at a time, until all the shortening is removed from the spoon. Stir the spoons for two minutes after adding each drop. How many drops of soap does it take to remove all the shortening?

You can expand this experiment by comparing different brands of soap. The brand that cleans the best is the one that takes the least amount of liquid soap to remove all the shortening from the spoon. Be sure that each experiment you do has only one independent variable—the brand of soap that you are testing. Thus, you must use identical spoons, the same amount of shortening and water, and keep the water temperature the same for all the soap brands you test.

Experiment 1.2
MAKING SOAP PATTERNS

Liquid soaps are very popular with consumers. For one thing, they can be conveniently pumped from a dispenser.

Fill a plastic bottle about one-quarter full with liquid soap that contains glycol stearate. Using a dropper, add five drops of food coloring. Fill the rest of the bottle to the very top with water by slowly running the water down the inner side of the bottle, as shown in Figure 2. Screw the cap on the bottle. Gently turn

Materials

* small, clear plastic bottle with screw cap (the rounder the bottle, the better the results)
* liquid soap that has glycol stearate as an ingredient
* dropper
* food coloring
* transparent tape

it upside down a few times to mix the soap and water, but try not to create soap bubbles. If you get soap bubbles inside the bottle, remove the cap and carefully pour off the foam. Add more water to the bottle. Replace the cap and dry the bottle. Wrap transparent tape around the cap so that the bottle will not leak.

Twist and shake the bottle to see what colored soap swirls and streaks you can make. Experiment by using different liquid soaps, mixing different food colorings, and changing the temperature of the water that you add to the plastic bottle. Which combination produces the most interesting swirls and streaks?

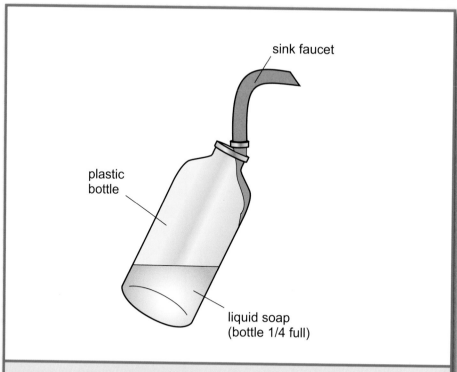

sink faucet

plastic
bottle

liquid soap
(bottle 1/4 full)

Figure 2. Tilt the plastic bottle under a sink faucet. Allow the water to flow very slowly down the inner side of the bottle.

The swirls and streaks that form in the plastic bottle make up something called a turbulence pattern. Turbulence is the random motion of fluids, like water and liquid soap. Turbulence in the oceans is responsible for bringing nutrients to the surface for small organisms to feed on. Turbulence in the air is responsible for weather patterns. Satellites can photograph the turbulence patterns that form in the atmosphere.

Check the library and Internet for information on turbulence. Try to locate information on what scientists hope to understand by studying turbulence. As part of your project, use this experiment to demonstrate and explain turbulence.

You may be familiar with one group of microorganisms called bacteria. Most people think that all bacteria cause disease in humans, but they do not all pose a health threat to humans. In fact, some types of bacteria are very beneficial. One such type of bacteria lives in your intestines. These bacteria make vitamin K, something you need to remain healthy.

However, most of the bacteria that enter your body can cause disease. These bacteria may cause tooth decay, ulcers, and even life-threatening diseases such as food poisoning and meningitis. Fortunately, the human body has several ways of killing these bacteria before they do any damage. There are also several lines of defense to prevent these bacteria from entering the body in the first place. The first line of defense is our skin.

Washing with soap and water keeps the skin clean and helps to wash away bacteria and other disease-causing microorganisms. Some liquid soaps even have an ingredient that kills bacteria. These soaps often include the word antibacterial on their labels. You can test how well these soaps kill bacteria with this experiment.

Materials

* an adult
* 2 small glass jars
* masking tape
* marker
* chicken broth
* teaspoon
* sugar
* liquid soap with an antibacterial ingredient
* liquid bleach
* pair of rubber or plastic kitchen gloves

Thoroughly clean two small glass jars with liquid soap and water. Be sure to rinse the jars thoroughly with running water. Label one jar *A*, the other *B*. Half fill both jars with chicken broth. Add one teaspoon of sugar to each jar. Stir the broth until the sugar dissolves. The chicken broth and sugar will provide the nutrients that bacteria need to grow and multiply.

Add one teaspoon of liquid soap to the jar labeled A and stir gently. Place both jars in a spot where they are exposed to the air. Bacteria in the air will fall into the open jars. If these bacteria start to grow and multiply, you will notice that the broth turns cloudy, as shown in Figure 3. Of course, if the liquid soap is effective, the broth should remain clear—or at least stay clear longer than the

chicken broth, sugar, and liquid soap

chicken broth and sugar

Figure 3. The cloudiness of the broth on the right is due to the growth of bacteria. These bacteria can even form solid clumps over time.

broth that has no liquid soap. Experiment to determine how much soap is needed to slow down or prevent the growth of bacteria. You can either add more soap at the beginning or add a little each day as your experiment progresses. Keep a record in your notebook.

If bacteria grow in the broth, be sure that you do not come in contact with the broth. Also be sure that none of the broth spills. The bacteria growing in the broth may be capable of causing disease. When you are finished with your broth, put on a pair of rubber or plastic kitchen gloves. **Under adult supervision**, fill each jar with liquid bleach. Allow the jars to remain undisturbed for 24 hours. The bleach will kill the bacteria. Once the bacteria have been killed, you can pour the contents down a drain and flush thoroughly with running water. Rinse the jars with running water. Wash them thoroughly with soap and warm water before using them to store any food or liquids.

Project Idea

Antibacterial Products

Liquid hand soap is not the only household product that contains ingredients that kill bacteria. Other products include hand lotions, dishwashing detergents, sponges, kitchen cutting boards, plastic wrap for foods, pillows, sheets, mattress pads, socks, athletic shoes, toothpastes, and even toys. The active ingredient in most of these products is an antibacterial chemical called triclosan. Triclosan is even added to the metal used to make small kitchen appliances such as toasters and mixers.

It would seem that bacteria do not stand a chance of surviving in a household equipped with all these products. In fact, using these products would seem to guarantee a germ-free household.

However, scientists have expressed a serious concern about the increasing number of household products that contain an antibacterial ingredient. One concern is that these products destroy good bacteria as well as those that cause disease. Another concern is that these products cannot kill all the harmful bacteria. Those that survive may produce immune strains that will pose a serious threat to human health in the future.

Carry out a project that lists all the household products that contain an antibacterial ingredient. How many of these products do you have in your home? With the help of a teacher or another adult, design an experiment that tests whether such a product does reduce the number of bacteria. You can base your design on Experiment 1.3. For example, brush your teeth first thing in the morning with a toothpaste that does not contain an antibacterial ingredient. Then wipe your teeth with a cotton swab. Next, stir the swab in chicken broth and sugar. Cover the liquid with foil and check if bacteria grow. Do the same the following morning with a toothpaste that contains an antibacterial ingredient. Does brushing with this toothpaste get rid of more bacteria?

Materials

* toothpaste
* several new glass microscope slides
* lens tissue
* hand lens or microscope
* tall narrow jar with lid
* clock

With the increased amount of sugars and soft foods in our diets, the incidence of tooth decay has risen sharply in many areas of the world. As a result, tooth decay has become the most common disease in the world. Nearly everyone will at some point in his or her life get tooth decay. This situation would be much worse if it were not for toothpaste.

Tooth decay is caused by a sticky substance called plaque. Plaque develops when bacteria in the mouth break down sugars on your teeth. The bacteria change the sugars into plaque, which destroys the enamel surface of teeth. As this enamel layer is gradually destroyed, a cavity forms. Brushing with toothpaste removes plaque found on the surface of teeth. To remove plaque, a toothpaste must be able to cause abrasion. Abrasion is simply the ability to remove something by rubbing it. The more abrasion a toothpaste can cause, the better it is at removing plaque. However, too much abrasion can damage tooth enamel. The ingredient in toothpaste that provides the abrasive action is called calcium carbonate.

Place a small dab of toothpaste on a new, clean glass microscope slide. Place another new slide on top. Gently rub the two slides back and forth 50 times. Remove the top slide and wash it with running water. Dry the slide with lens tissue. Examine the slide under a microscope or with a hand lens. If there are only a few scratches on the slide, then rate the abrasive action of the toothpaste as light. If the slide has many scratches, then rate it as heavy. Anything in between would be rated as moderate abrasive action. It will be easier to tell the difference between light, moderate, and heavy abrasion if you carry out this experiment with different brands of toothpaste. Just be sure to treat each brand in exactly the same way so that you have only one independent variable.

Toothpastes also contain an ingredient called sodium lauryl sulfate to clean the teeth. You can check the cleansing action of a toothpaste by placing some in a tall narrow jar. Use an amount equal to what you would put on a toothbrush. Half fill the jar with water. Put the lid on the jar and shake vigorously for one minute. A toothpaste that cleans well will foam easily. Repeat this procedure to check different toothpaste brands for their cleansing action.

Project Idea

Fluorides in Toothpaste

The ingredient in toothpaste that provides the abrasive action is called calcium carbonate. The soap that is added to toothpaste is usually sodium lauryl sulfate. You probably have not heard of either of these ingredients. But you probably have heard of one of the other ingredients in toothpaste—fluoride. Fluoride hardens the enamel surface of teeth. Thus, fluoride helps prevent tooth decay. But the fluoride in toothpaste can be a serious problem for children under the age of six. These children can develop a condition known as fluorosis. Once fluorosis occurs, it will not go away.

Check the library or the Internet for information on fluorosis, especially as to why young children are most likely to develop it. Also check how the Food and Drug Administration (FDA) and the American Dental Association (ADA) have addressed this problem. Finally, take a close look at the label on a package of toothpaste. What warning does it provide for children under the age of six?

Locate information on "natural" toothpastes. As part of your project, make your own fluoride-free toothpaste and check its abrasive and cleansing actions. You can locate recipes for making toothpaste on the Internet. One simple recipe calls for mixing three parts bicarbonate of soda with one part salt. Add three teaspoons of glycerine for every quarter cup of this mixture. Add enough water to make a thick paste. Add a few drops of peppermint oil for taste. Mix well and start brushing!

Experiment 1.5

EVALUATING SHAMPOOS

All shampoos contain an ingredient that cleans hair by allowing the oils and grease to mix with water. This ingredient is actually a detergent. Chapter 5 will look at detergents and discuss how they differ from soaps. The detergent in shampoos causes the natural oil in hair, known as sebum, to mix with water so that the dirt can be washed away. Because all shampoos contain a detergent, all brands can get hair clean. If this is the case, can one brand of shampoo be any better than another? Carry out this experiment with at least two different shampoo brands to find the answer. If possible, compare an expensive brand to an inexpensive brand.

Materials

* shampoo (at least 2 different brands)
* measuring cup
* large bowl
* large spoon
* tall, narrow glass jar with lid
* ruler
* India ink
* dropper
* tall, narrow glass container (bud vase works well)
* small marble or tiny steel ball bearing
* clock or stopwatch

Prepare a one percent solution of each brand of shampoo. To do this, dilute 1 fluid ounce of the shampoo with 99 fluid ounces of water in a large bowl. Use a large spoon to mix the shampoo gently to avoid producing soap bubbles. Pour 2 fluid ounces of the diluted shampoo into a tall, narrow glass jar. To avoid producing any foam, pour the diluted shampoo down the inner side of the jar.

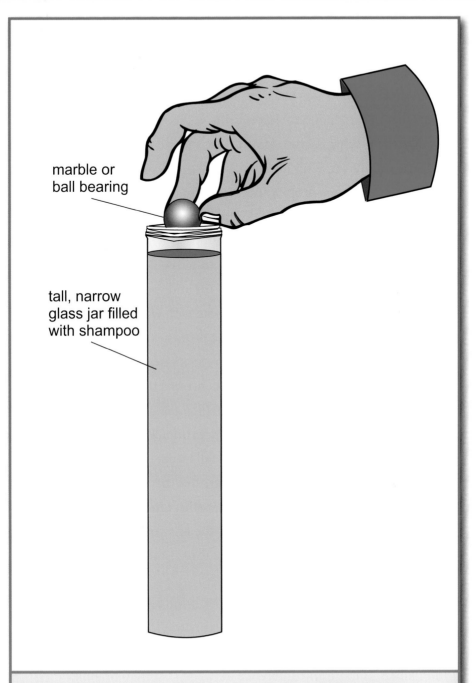

marble or
ball bearing

tall, narrow
glass jar filled
with shampoo

Figure 4. Gently place a ball bearing or small marble on the
surface. Time how long it takes for it to fall to the bottom.

Screw the lid on the jar. Measure the height of the shampoo. Shake the jar vigorously ten times. Measure the height of the foam. A good shampoo will produce at least twice its volume in foam when shaken ten times. Thus, the height of the foam should be twice that of the shampoo. Repeat this procedure three times and average the results. Each time, rinse the jar and use fresh solution.

Rinse out the jar. Pour another 2 fluid ounces of diluted shampoo into the jar. Add one drop of India ink, put the lid on the jar, and shake ten times. Look to see if the India ink has spread out in the liquid, in the foam, or both. Good shampoos will cause solids, such as dirt and India ink, to spread out in the liquid. This way the dirt can be washed away with water. Dirt and grease trapped in the foam are more difficult to wash away with water. Repeat this procedure three times and average the results.

The "body" of a shampoo is known as its viscosity. The higher the viscosity, the thicker or more concentrated the shampoo. To determine the viscosity of a shampoo, fill a tall, narrow, glass container with undiluted shampoo. Determine the time it takes for a small marble or tiny ball bearing to fall to the bottom of the glass container, as shown in Figure 4. The greater the viscosity of the shampoo, the longer it will take for the object to fall to the bottom. The more concentrated the shampoo, the less you may need to clean your hair. Repeat this procedure three times and average the results.

Compare your results for the two shampoo brands you tested for their ability to foam, their ability to wash away dirt, and their viscosity. Summarize your findings in a chart, such as the one shown in Figure 5. Is there any difference between shampoo brands? When you are finished with the experiment, pour any unused shampoo back into the original bottle.

Shampoo Brand	Foam	Dirt	Viscosity
Brand 1	3 times height of liquid	in liquid	3.5 seconds
Brand 2	same height as liquid	in foam	1.5 seconds

Average test results for shampoo's ability to foam and wash dirt, and its viscosity

Figure 5. Making a table is a good way to summarize the data you collect in your experiments. Based on the data in the table, which brand of shampoo would you buy? Why?

Chapter 2

MAKING YOU LOOK GOOD

You now know that personal products to prevent disease were not considered important until less than two hundred years ago. But looking good was recognized long before then! About four thousand years ago, people began to apply certain products to improve their personal appearance. The ancient Egyptians were among the first people to use cosmetics. Egyptian men, women, and children colored their lips and cheeks, stained their nails, and lined their eyes and eyebrows.

The walls of Egyptian tombs are covered with portraits of people wearing brightly colored cosmetics, especially reds, blues, and greens. The Egyptians were known to use colored materials found in nature to make their cosmetics. For example, they crushed the reddish flowers of a shrub called henna to make nail polish. They used minerals with a high copper content to make green eye shadow.

Jars containing these cosmetics were found in the 1800s by French archaeologists who were excavating Egyptian tombs. These jars were taken to the Louvre, a museum in Paris, where they remained undisturbed for over 150 years. Then in 1999, French scientists decided to take a closer look at the contents of these jars. To their surprise, many of the products contained ingredients that do not exist in nature. In other words, the Egyptians did not rely entirely on natural products to get their cosmetic ingredients. They also made their own cosmetic ingredients. These Egyptians could be considered ancient scientists who had experimented with ways of making cosmetic products that everyone could use.

In addition to using cosmetic products, the Egyptians also used perfumes. Unlike cosmetic products, however, perfumes were a luxury item for the Egyptians. These expensive perfumes were stored in elaborate glass bottles for use mainly by the members of the royal family and wealthy people. Many of these perfume bottles were also sent by ship to other countries, where they were sold to those who could afford them. Egyptian perfumes were especially valuable because they were known to keep their scent for as long as twenty years. If these perfumes could have kept their scent for four thousand years, you may have recognized some of them.

RECOGNIZING SCENTS

People like not only to be clean but also to smell nice. A person may want to smell fresh, spicy, or floral. Baby powder can give someone a fresh smell; an aftershave lotion can make a person smell spicy; perfumes can lend a floral scent. Have you ever wondered how you can distinguish between all these different fragrances, or smells?

Your nose is lined with about 5 million cells that carry out a specialized job. These cells can detect various odors that are carried by the air. Each of these cells is covered by tiny hairs. These hairs have places into which certain chemical substances can fit. When just the right substances occupy these places, the nose cell sends a message to the brain. The brain then interprets the message as a particular odor. In fact, the brain can recognize up to ten thousand different odors. The following experiment will give you the opportunity to see how well the brains of your family members and friends can recognize different odors.

Materials

* large round coffee filter
* scissors
* bath powder
* fresh-scented underarm deodorant (with baking soda)
* lime-scented shaving cream
* mint-flavored toothpaste
* 4 plastic freezer bags
* marking pen
* 4 volunteers
* unscented facial tissues

Cut a large round coffee filter into four equal-sized pieces, as shown in Figure 6. Rub or sprinkle each personal care product—bath powder, deodorant, shaving cream, and toothpaste—onto a separate piece of the filter. Be sure that you place enough of the product on the filter so that a distinct odor is noticeable. Place each piece into a separate plastic freezer bag. Seal and label each bag with a letter. Record what product each letter represents.

Have each of your volunteer subjects open one plastic bag at a time. Ask them to smell and identify the odor that has been put onto the coffee filter. Inform your subjects that they can identify either the product or the particular odor that it produces. Be sure

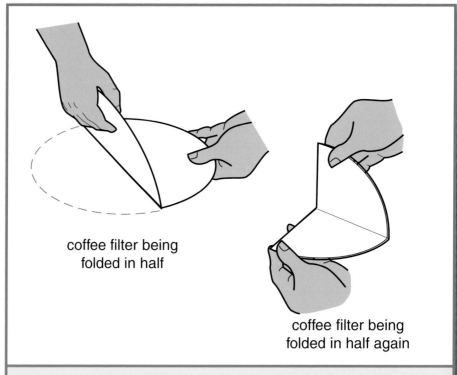

coffee filter being
folded in half

coffee filter being
folded in half again

Figure 6. Fold a coffee filter in half, and then in half again. Open the filter and cut along the fold marks to get four equal-sized pieces.

that they do not touch or remove the filter. Have the person breathe through an unscented facial tissue before smelling the next odor. In this way, the person will clear any remaining odor before smelling the next one. Keep a list to record which odors each person correctly and incorrectly identifies. Was there one odor that most of your subjects could not identify? Was there one that everyone could identify? How can you explain the results of your experiment?

Project Idea

Aromatherapy

Aromatherapy is the use of certain odors to promote health and healing. The healing properties are claimed to come from concentrated solutions prepared from herbs, flowers, and other types of plants. These solutions are known as essential oils. Geranium is an essential oil that is used to ease stress. The odors that these essential oils produce are inhaled directly or with the help of vaporizers.

Check the library and the Internet for information on aromatherapy. Other key terms to use in your research are holistic medicine, holistic health, and essential oils. Based on your research, select one specific odor (essential oil) in a project designed to determine if the odor does what it is supposed to do. For example, marjoram is recommended for people who have insomnia. If you can identify people who have serious trouble sleeping, perhaps they would be willing to serve as subjects in a project aimed at finding out if marjoram helps them sleep better. Be sure to work under adult supervision in designing and carrying out your project. Follow the guidelines on how the essential oil should be used.

Do not forget that your project design must have only one independent variable for each subject—the essential oil that you are testing. Thus, each of your subjects must agree to follow the same routine, eat the same foods, perform the same amount of exercise, etc. before going to bed each night. Your subject must then evaluate how well he or she slept those nights when aromatherapy was used before going to bed.

Experiment 2.2
Comparing Skin Lotions

People spend billions of dollars each year on cosmetic products to smell nice or not to smell; to straighten hair or make it curl; to dry skin or add moisture to it. Many people will spend a considerable amount of money on a cosmetic product, believing that it works wonders. However, what most consumers do not realize is that the cost of the chemical ingredients used to make a cosmetic product is a small fraction of the retail price. Most of the price of a cosmetic product covers research and development, advertising costs, and the manufacturer's and store's overhead and profits.

Materials

* measuring spoons
* honey
* vegetable oil
* lemon juice
* small glass jar
* commercial skin lotion
* plastic wrap
* incandescent light

Let's take a look at one cosmetic product you can probably find at home: skin lotion. These lotions are sold for a variety of purposes. Most claim to add moisture to dry skin. Many contain vitamins and special ingredients to promote healing. Some offer protection against harmful rays from the sun. These lotions are usually made by mixing oil with water. But as you know, oil and water do not mix. Thus, the manufacturer adds a third ingredient, called an emulsifier, that allows the oil and water to mix. Also, a chemical is added to prevent the growth of bacteria. Some type of perfume is

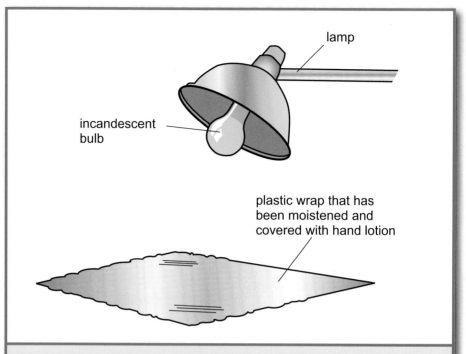

lamp

incandescent bulb

plastic wrap that has been moistened and covered with hand lotion

Figure 7. Be sure to use a light source that gives off heat, such as an incandescent bulb. You can also place the plastic wrap in direct sunlight.

used to produce a pleasant scent. But the main ingredient in hand lotion is water.

You can use some ingredients you probably have at home to make a hand lotion. You can then compare your inexpensive lotion to a commercial brand that you may have at home. Based on your results, you may decide never to purchase another skin lotion but rather to use your homemade product.

To prepare your skin lotion, mix one tablespoon of honey, one tablespoon of vegetable oil, and half a teaspoon of lemon juice in a glass jar. Be sure that the jar has been thoroughly cleaned and dried. Apply the mixture to the back of one of your hands. Apply the same amount of a commercial skin lotion to the back of your other hand. After ten minutes, rinse your hands in warm water. Do not scrub your hands or use soap, as you will wash off your lotions.

Rate each lotion as far as its effectiveness in softening or adding moisture to your skin. Compare the softness of your skin to an area where you did not apply any lotion. Score each lotion with a 0, +, ++, or +++. If no softening effect can be detected, then the lotion would receive a 0 rating. If the lotion adds a lot of moisture, then rate it as +++.

For a less subjective test, mix up another batch of your homemade lotion. Soak a piece of plastic wrap in water for a few minutes. Then cut the plastic wrap into two equal-sized pieces and spread them out on a countertop. Spread your homemade lotion so that it lightly covers one of the pieces. Cover the other piece of plastic wrap with the commercial skin lotion. Place both pieces of plastic wrap under an incandescent light, as shown in Figure 7. The wrap should be slightly wrinkled. Note how long it takes for them to dry. Was one lotion more effective in preventing the water from evaporating?

Experiment 2.3

CLEANING WITH A CREAM

Cold cream or cleansing creams are used to remove oily deposits and grease left by makeup. Like skin lotions, cold creams are made from an oil-water mixture. The ratio of oil to water determines how thick the cream will be. You can find cold creams that are liquids and some that are thick creams. When applied to the skin, the oil and water in the cream separate. The water evaporates, producing a cooling effect on the skin. The oil dissolves any grease deposits from makeup, which can then be wiped away with a tissue or towel. In this experiment, you can make your own cold cream and then check how well it

works against a commercial product in getting rid of the grease left by makeup.

Make sure that all the equipment you use is thoroughly clean. To make your own cold cream, combine one egg yolk and two tablespoons of lemon juice in a small bowl. Stir with a wire whisk while slowly adding a half cup of olive oil and a half cup of vegetable oil. The egg yolk-lemon juice mixture should thicken as you add the oils. If the mixture is too thick, add more lemon juice.

Materials

* egg
* lemon juice
* olive oil
* vegetable oil
* measuring spoon
* measuring cup
* small bowl
* wire whisk
* lipstick
* commercial cold cream
* assorted cosmetic products
* facial tissues or cotton balls

Rub lipstick on the back of each hand. Apply about a tablespoon of your homemade cold cream to one hand and an equal amount of a commercial product to your other hand. Follow the directions on the container to remove the lipstick with the commercial cold cream. Follow the same procedure to see how well your homemade cold cream works in removing the lipstick. **Do not use your homemade cold cream on your lips, as raw egg can cause illness. Wash your hands thoroughly.** You can repeat this procedure to check how well your cold creams remove other cosmetic products such as eye shadows and makeup foundations.

Experiment 2.4
PREPARING A TALCUM POWDER

Clothing can stick to the skin, and this is really true on hot, humid days. To prevent this from happening, some people apply body powder. The one most commonly used is talcum powder. This type of powder gets its name from its main ingredient—talc.

Talc is actually a mineral. Its scientific name is magnesium silicate hydroxide. Talc has a number of uses other than in talcum powder. Because it is resistant to heat and electricity, talc is ideal for making laboratory countertops. But its usefulness as a powder comes from another of talc's properties. Talc is one of the softest minerals known. In 1812, a German scientist named Friedrich Mohs developed a scale of mineral hardness. Talc was rated as the softest mineral, with the lowest Mohs' hardness rating of 1. Table 2 lists some minerals and common household items along with their Mohs' hardness ratings. Which substance is the hardest?

Because of its softness, talc can be ground into very small particles to make a powder. These fine particles produce tiny slippery plates that glide over each other. This reduces friction and thus

> ## Materials
>
> * baking soda
> * cornstarch
> * measuring cup
> * fragrance oil
> * dropper
> * bowl
> * wooden stirrer
> * large plastic bottle
> * plastic wrap
> * rubber band
> * toothpick
> * commercial talc-free powder
> * several adult volunteers

Substance	Mohs' Hardness Rating
talc	1
gypsum	2
fingernail	2.5
copper penny	3
fluorite	4
glass	5.5
metal file	6.5
quartz	7
topaz	8
diamond	10

Table 2. Mohs' hardness ratings for various substances

prevents the skin from becoming irritated by clothing that might otherwise stick. The fine powder that is produced by the tiny particles of talc also absorbs moisture. But the fine powder also poses a possible health hazard, especially to young children.

The tiny talc particles can remain suspended in the air. These particles can be inhaled into the lungs, where they can cause problems with breathing. There have been many reports of babies having life-threatening episodes from inhaling powder. In fact, a number of babies have died because of breathing problems brought about by inhaling talcum powder. As a result, the labels on baby powders have a warning to keep the powder away from a child's face. Some doctors recommend that parents use an ointment rather

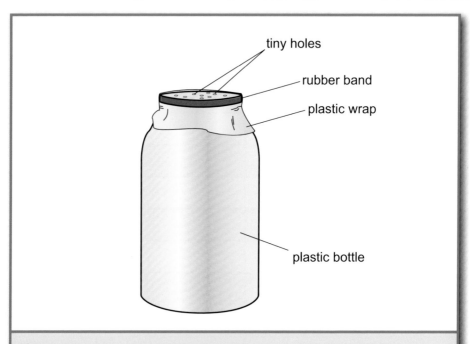

Figure 8. Store your powder in a clean, dry plastic bottle. Cover the opening with plastic wrap and secure it with a rubber band. Punch tiny holes in the plastic wrap so that you can shake out the powder when you need it.

than baby powder to prevent and treat diaper rash. For those who still use a powder for their babies, a talc-free or "dustless" powder is recommended. You can make your own talc-free powder in this experiment and test it against a commercial product.

Combine a half cup of baking soda and a half cup of cornstarch in a bowl. Mix them together until they are thoroughly blended. Add about 20 drops of a fragrance oil to the powder and mix thoroughly. Allow the powder to dry in the bowl. Store it in a large plastic bottle covered with plastic wrap, as shown in Figure 8. Using a toothpick, poke tiny holes in the plastic wrap. You are now ready to field test your homemade "dustless" powder against a commercial product.

Assemble a group of adults to serve as volunteers. The best time of the year to conduct your study would be the hot, humid months in the summer, but you can still evaluate the effectiveness of each powder at other times of the year. You may just have to ask your volunteers to work up a sweat.

Ask each person to apply some of your homemade powder to the right side of their upper body and the commercial brand of talc-free powder to the left side. Have your subjects rate how each powder performs in terms of making them feel fresh and preventing skin irritation. Does your powder work better with any particular type of clothing?

Project Idea

Polymers

Talcum powder can be used to make some interesting chemical substances known as polymers. The prefix *poly* means "many." The suffix *-mer* refers to a building block used to make a chemical. A monomer, for example, is made of only one of these building blocks. In contrast, a polymer is made of many of these building blocks strung together into a long chain. Figure 9 illustrates how a polymer is made from monomers.

To make a polymer, combine 25 mL of white glue and 20 mL of water in a paper cup. Add one teaspoon of talcum powder. Mix these ingredients thoroughly. Add 5 mL of a detergent containing borax and stir to make your polymer. You can make another polymer by combining two teaspoons of an oil-free moisturizing lotion, two teaspoons of white glue, two teaspoons of water, and one teaspoon of talcum powder in a paper cup. Mix these ingredients thoroughly. Add one teaspoon of detergent and stir to make your

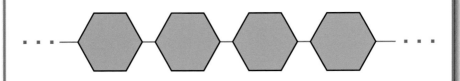

Figure 9. Each of these four chemicals is a monomer. Hundreds, or even thousands, of monomers may be joined to form a single polymer.

polymer. Experiment by varying the proportions of the ingredients to see how this affects the polymer you make.

Check the library and the Internet for information on polymers and the different ways they are made. Some valuable polymers were first made purely by accident. These include the vulcanized rubber that is used to make tires; Bakelite, which is found on billiard balls and telephones; and nylon, which is woven to make stockings. Prepare a report summarizing your findings on polymers. What other polymers can you make to include as part of your report?

Experiment 2.5
HOLDING ON TO WATER

You read that one use of talcum powder is to prevent and treat diaper rash. At one time, using diapers was most unappealing—until disposable diapers came along. No longer did parents have to wash out soiled diapers so that they could be reused. Now they could simply toss out the dirty diaper and get a new one. If there is a baby in your house—or if you know someone with a baby—ask for a clean disposable diaper to use in this experiment.

Materials

* disposable diapers
* kitchen scale
* large bowl
* wooden stirrer
* sheet of newspaper
* small glass jar

Weigh the clean, dry diaper on a kitchen scale. Place the diaper in a large bowl. Cover the diaper with water and allow it to soak for five minutes, stirring occasionally. If the diaper becomes exposed as it absorbs water, add more water to keep it covered. Remove the diaper from the bowl and hold it over a sink. Wait until the water has stopped dripping. Then weigh the wet diaper on the kitchen scale. Determine how much water the diaper can hold by subtracting the weight of the dry diaper from the weight of the wet diaper:

$$\text{weight of water in diaper} = \text{weight of wet diaper} - \text{weight of dry diaper}$$

Check with family and friends to see if they can give you a different brand of diaper to test. Does one brand absorb more water than any other brand?

Take another diaper apart to find out what actually absorbs the water. Continue to pull apart each layer until you reach a layer of cotton. This cotton layer contains small crystals. Pull out some of the cotton from this layer and shake it over a sheet of newspaper. You should hear the crystals drop on the paper. Try to collect as many crystals as possible without getting too much of the cotton fibers. Weigh the crystals and then transfer them to a small glass jar. Cover the crystals with a known amount of water and stir. Describe what happens to the solid crystals. Determine how much water these crystals can absorb.

Project Idea

Solid Wastes and Recycling

Disposable diapers may have been welcomed by most parents, especially those who used cloth diapers that had to be washed. But cloth diapers have one advantage over disposable diapers. Cloth diapers can be washed and reused many times before they wear out and have to be discarded. Obviously, disposable diapers are used just once. Thus, disposable diapers have added to the problem of solid wastes.

Design a project that looks at the impact of disposable diapers on solid wastes in your local community. Determine what percentage of solid wastes is due to disposable diapers. You can ask a family who uses disposable diapers to help in your project. They can place all the diapers in a trash bag separate from all the other solid wastes they toss. Weighing all this garbage will reveal the percent that disposable diapers contribute to solid wastes in the household. You can project your findings based on one family to what is happening in your local community. As part of your project, include information on how your community deals with solid waste disposal and recycling. Your project results may provide a reason for parents to go back to cloth diapers.

Are there any ecological drawbacks to using cloth diapers? Research the question to find out.

Chapter 3

HERE'S TO YOUR HEALTH

Have you ever heard of the disease called scurvy? It is a conditiona caused by a lack of vitamin C. In 1781 a regiment of about eight hundred British soldiers sailed for India. After nearly a year at sea, the regiment finally reached their destination. By that time, 121 soldiers had died from scurvy. The first visible sign of this disease is red spots that appear on the legs, arms, and back. A person with scurvy soon becomes weak and develops pain in the joints. Internal bleeding produces black-and-blue marks. The gums become so soft that teeth easily fall out. Eating becomes difficult and painful.

In 1747 a British doctor named James Lind conducted a study of twelve people who had scurvy. He evenly divided the twelve people into two groups—a control group and an experimental group. Those in the experimental group were given lemons and oranges to eat. These six people recovered from scurvy. However, the six people in the control group who were not given fruit did not recover.

Lind later discovered that limes were just as effective as lemons and oranges in preventing scurvy. He seemed to have found the cure for this disease—35 years before the deaths of those 121

British soldiers and thousands of others on long sea voyages. But it took Lind 41 years to convince the British Royal Navy that he had found a cure for scurvy. In 1795 the British Royal Navy finally required that all its sailors drink some lime juice every day. For this reason, British sailors became known as limeys.

In the 1880s a Japanese doctor named Kanehiro Takaki was investigating another disease. Takaki was trying to find out why almost half of Japanese sailors were developing beriberi. The first signs of beriberi include overall weakness, followed by a loss of feeling in the feet and legs. The body then swells up because of fluids that collect inside. If a person does not recover from beriberi, the heart may stop working.

Takaki observed that Japanese sailors were being given a high proportion of rice in their daily rations. He found that replacing some of this rice with vegetables, fish, and meat prevented beriberi. Soon after Takaki's findings, the Japanese Navy required that all its sailors follow his diet. In six years, beriberi was no longer a health threat to Japanese sailors.

In 1913 Joseph Goldberger began to investigate the cause of still another disease. Known as pellagra, this disease was quickly becoming an epidemic in several southern U.S. states. Pellagra causes skin rashes, mouth sores, and diarrhea. If a person does not recover, pellagra can affect the brain. Goldberger investigated the cause of pellagra by working with inmates who were serving time for minor crimes in a Mississippi prison. Those who volunteered to take part in his experiment would get a pardon.

Half the prison volunteers made up the control group. These inmates continued to eat the usual prison food, which was well balanced. The other half in the experimental group were given a diet that was typical of what poor people in the South were eating—cornbread, molasses, and a little pork fat. Within months, those in the experimental group developed pellagra. The symptoms of the disease disappeared when the inmates were given meat, fresh vegetables, and milk.

What all these studies had shown was the value of eating the right foods. What Lind, Takaki, and Goldberger did not know was that the right foods contain substances that the body needs to stay healthy. Without these substances, diseases such as scurvy, beriberi, and pellagra may set in. These substances are vitamins. A balanced diet should provide all the vitamins the body needs to stay healthy. Today, vitamins are only one of the health care products that people regularly use.

Testing for Vitamin C

Many people do not make the effort to eat foods that supply enough of the vitamins they need. They sometimes rely on fast foods that provide little, if any, nutritional value. Moreover, frozen, canned, and pre-cooked foods—which many people favor—contain greatly reduced levels of vitamins. To make up for the loss of vitamins in their food, more and more people are taking vitamin supplements on a regular basis.

Materials

* measuring cup
* large glass jar
* spray starch
* Lugol's solution
* dropper
* small glass jar
* vitamin C tablet
* wax paper
* large spoon or small hammer
* orange juice

One vitamin that many people take in large doses is vitamin C. The scientific name for vitamin C is ascorbic acid. Vitamin C is required for healthy bones and gums. It is also needed for the growth and repair of body tissues. One consequence of not getting enough vitamin C is scurvy.

An alternative to taking vitamin C tablets is to drink plenty of fruit juices and to eat citrus fruits, such as lemons, oranges, and limes. These juices and fruits are rich in vitamin C. This experiment will show you how to find out which brand of orange juice contains the most vitamin C.

Pour 1 cup of cold water into a large glass jar. Squirt some spray starch into the water. Swirl gently to dissolve the starch. Add ten drops of Lugol's solution. Almost every biology or life science classroom has Lugol's solution for staining specimens to view under a microscope. Ask a science teacher for a small bottle. Be careful not to spill the Lugol's solution, as it will stain your hands and clothes. The color of the starch solution should be royal blue. If it is not, add more Lugol's solution.

Pour 1 fluid ounce of the starch-iodine solution into a small glass jar. To see what happens when vitamin C is added to this solution, fold a vitamin C tablet inside a piece of wax paper. Crush it by pressing down with a large spoon or small hammer. Dissolve the crushed vitamin C in 1 cup of water. Add a drop of the vitamin C solution to the starch-iodine solution, as shown in Figure 10.

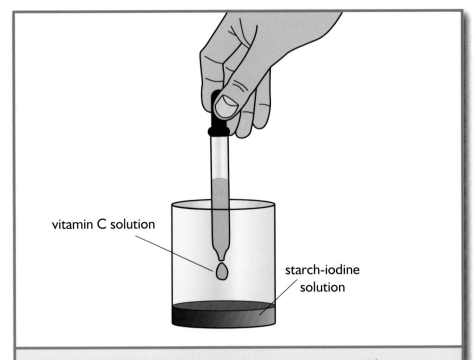

vitamin C solution

starch-iodine
solution

Figure 10. Hold the dropper straight up and down. In this way, the drops will all be about the same size. Swirl the starch-iodine solution after adding each drop.

Gently swirl the liquids so that they mix thoroughly. Continue adding the vitamin C solution drop by drop until the starch-iodine solution turns from royal blue to colorless. Be sure that you swirl the starch solution after adding each drop.

Lugol's solution combines with starch to form a royal blue color. Vitamin C, however, has a greater attraction than starch for Lugol's solution. Vitamin C combines with Lugol's solution to produce a colorless solution. As you continue to add drops of vitamin C solution, more and more Lugol's solution is removed from the starch. Once all the Lugol's solution has been stripped from the starch, the solution becomes colorless.

Now check to see if your orange juice has vitamin C. Thoroughly clean the glass jar and again add 1 fluid ounce of the starch-iodine solution. This time, add the orange juice, drop by drop, until the starch solution turns colorless. If the juice does not contain any vitamin C, then the starch solution will not turn colorless. Rather the solution will begin to take on the color of the juice. In this case, you can say that the juice did not contain any measurable amount of vitamin C.

By keeping track of how much juice you add, you can test different brands of orange juices to determine which one has the most vitamin C. The less juice you add to turn the starch-iodine solution colorless, the more vitamin C it contains. You can also check out other juices and fresh fruits and vegetables for their vitamin C content. But first you will have to squeeze the juice from the fruits or liquefy them in a blender.

Project Idea

Stability of Vitamin C

Vitamin C is not very stable. In other words, vitamin C breaks down easily. Carry out a project designed to test how temperature, light, and exposure to the air affect the stability of vitamin C. You can use either a solution prepared with a vitamin C tablet or a juice that you find contains a high vitamin C concentration. Check out whether both cooling and heating cause vitamin C to break down. Is there one temperature at which vitamin C is most stable? When testing the effect of light on the stability of vitamin C, be sure to vary the amount of light to which the juice or solution is exposed. Check out whether all types of light (incandescent, fluorescent, halogen, sun, etc.) produce the same results.

Experiment 3.2
PRESERVING THE FRESHNESS OF FRUITS

Vitamin C not only plays a role in good health, it can also keep fruit fresh. You have probably noticed that apples, pears, bananas, and other fruits darken when they are peeled and exposed to air for a short time. Chemicals in these fruits react with oxygen. This reaction destroys cells in the fruit, causing them to turn brown. Vitamin C can slow down the reaction between the chemicals in the fruit and the oxygen in the air. As a result, the color and taste of the fruit are preserved. This is why chefs often squeeze a lemon or lime, which

Materials

* vitamin C tablet
* wax paper
* large spoon or small hammer
* large glass jar
* measuring cup
* various fruits
* knife
* paper cups
* paper towels
* clock
* orange juice

contain vitamin C, over a salad that contains freshly cut apples. In this experiment, you can determine if vitamin C is more effective in keeping one particular type of fruit fresh.

Fold a vitamin C tablet in a piece of wax paper. Crush the tablet by pressing down with a large spoon or small hammer. Transfer the crushed tablet to a large glass jar and dissolve it in 1 cup of water.

Obtain a variety of fruits, such as an apple, pear, and banana. Peel or skin each fruit. Cut two sections from each fruit and place each section in a different paper cup. All the sections should be the same size. Cover one set of fruit sections with the vitamin C solution.

Be sure that you add the same volume of vitamin C solution to each fruit section. Cover the other set of fruit sections with plain water as a control group.

After five minutes, pour the solution and water down a drain. Blot the fruit sections with a paper towel. Place the sections on a clean paper towel. Note how long it takes for each section to begin to turn brown. Repeat the experiment several times. Record your data in a table like the one shown in Figure 11.

You can test orange juices to see if they are as effective as a vitamin C solution in preserving the freshness of fruits. This would be an indirect way of determining which juice contains the most vitamin C. The more vitamin C in a juice, the more effective it should be in keeping fruit from turning brown when exposed to air.

Trial	Time elapsed before turning brown		
	Apple	Pear	Banana
1			
2			
3			

Figure 11. Like a scientist, you should not make any conclusions until you have repeated an experiment several times.

Experiment 3.3
Dissolving a Vitamin Tablet

Vitamins B1, B2, B3, B5, B6, B12, and C dissolve in water; they are water-soluble. In contrast, other vitamins do not dissolve in water. These include vitamins A, D, E, and K. These vitamins dissolve in oils and fats; they are lipid-soluble. If you did Experiment 1.1, then you saw that water and grease, which is a fat, do not mix. Thus, it makes sense that vitamins that dissolve in water will not dissolve in oil or fat, and vice versa.

If you crush a vitamin C tablet and then add it to water, the powder dissolves. The vitamin C particles become so small as they dissolve that you can no longer see them. The vitamin C is a solute. A solute is the substance that dissolves to form a solution. The water is a solvent. A solvent is the substance in which a solute dissolves to form a solution. In this experiment, you will examine how temperature affects the amount of solute that can dissolve in a solvent.

Fold a water-soluble vitamin tablet in a piece of wax paper. Crush it with a large spoon or a small hammer. Transfer the crushed tablet

Materials

* an adult
* 10 identical water-soluble vitamin B or C tablets
* wax paper
* large spoon or small hammer
* large glass jar
* glass measuring cup
* small pot
* oven mitt
* stove
* refrigerator
* alcohol thermometer, $-10\degree C-110\degree C$

66

to a large glass jar. Fill a glass measuring cup with water. Record the temperature of the water. Slowly add the water to the crushed tablet while stirring. Be sure that you add only a little water at a time. Determine the volume of water that you must add to dissolve all of the crushed tablet. To do this, subtract the volume of water remaining in the measuring cup from the volume you started with. Record the volume in your notebook.

Clean out and dry the measuring cup. Crush another vitamin tablet and place it in the cup. This time, pour some water into a small pot. **Under adult supervision**, heat the water on the stove so that the temperature increases 10 degrees Fahrenheit over that of the water used earlier. Using an oven mitt, slowly pour the heated water over the crushed tablet in the measuring cup. Record the volume of water that you must add to dissolve all of the tablet. This time the volume can be read right from the measuring cup.

Repeat this procedure using four additional water samples, each 10 degrees Fahrenheit warmer than the previous one. Be sure to wear an oven mitt when pouring these water samples. Record how much water must be added in each case to dissolve a crushed vitamin tablet.

Place some water in a refrigerator or freezer so that its temperature falls 10 degrees Fahrenheit below that of the water you first used. Repeat the above procedure using four additional water samples, each 10 degrees Fahrenheit cooler than the previous one. Again determine how much water is needed in each case to dissolve a crushed vitamin tablet.

Plot your results on a graph like the one shown in Figure 12. How does the temperature affect the amount of solvent that is needed to dissolve a water-soluble vitamin tablet? Not all substances dissolve the same way. You can expand this experiment

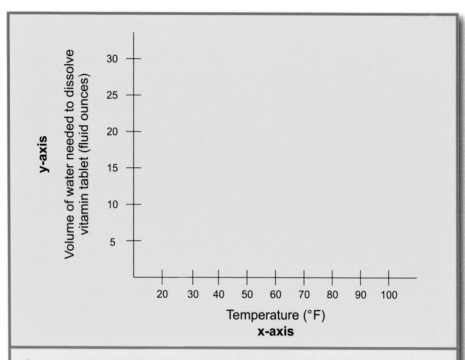

y-axis

Volume of water needed to dissolve vitamin tablet (fluid ounces)

30

25

20

15

10

5

20 30 40 50 60 70 80 90 100

Temperature (°F)

x-axis

Figure 12. The independent variable is plotted on the *x*-axis, while the dependent variable is plotted on the *y*-axis. Volume depends on temperature; volume is the dependent variable.

to see if the other water-soluble vitamins behave the same way as the vitamin you used. Comparing the graphs you get will give you the answer. Just be sure to use the same amount of vitamin in each experiment. In this way, the only independent variable in each experiment will be the water temperature.

Project Idea

Danger of Vitamin Overdosing

A person can much more easily overdose on a lipid-soluble vitamin than on a water-soluble vitamin. Any excess vitamin C and vitamin B that a person consumes dissolves in the watery part of blood called the plasma. These excess vitamins are transported to the kidneys, which eliminates them from the body. In contrast, lipid-soluble vitamins are stored in the fat of the liver. Over time, stored vitamins may cause fat deposits to build up in the liver and interfere with its functions.

Lipid-soluble vitamins, like vitamin A, are present in foods in only small amounts. Thus, it is usually impossible to consume too much of these vitamins. However, some people take large quantities of vitamin tablets on a daily basis. Large doses of lipid-soluble vitamins, if taken over a long time, can overload the liver and cause health problems. For example, large doses of vitamin A taken by pregnant women can lead to birth defects.

Carry out a project that is aimed at alerting consumers about the dangers of taking too many lipid-soluble vitamins over time. Include information about each vitamin and its possible effect on a person's health if taken in large quantities for too long. As part of your project, test if the vitamin has some adverse affect on a living creature other than a human or other vertebrate. For example, you can investigate the

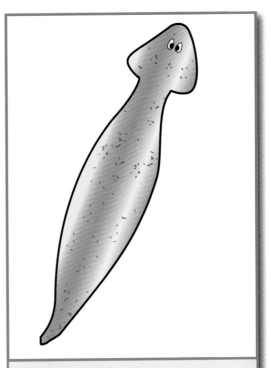

Figure 13. A planarian, a freshwater flatworm, can be used to see if large doses of vitamins affect its ability to regenerate lost parts.

vitamin's effect on a freshwater worm called a planarian, which is shown in Figure 13. These animals have an amazing ability to regenerate lost parts. Your project can investigate whether high doses of a lipid-soluble vitamin affect their ability to regenerate. But first you must work out a way of getting the lipid-soluble vitamin to dissolve in the water. You could dissolve the vitamin in vegetable oil, then use a liquid soap to disperse the oil in water, but be sure to set up the proper control to check out if soap or oil alone has any effect on regeneration.

Experiment 3.4

PROTECTING YOURSELF AGAINST THE SUN

Sunscreens absorb ultraviolet rays. Sunblocks actually deflect or turn away ultraviolet rays. Sunscreens contain chemicals that react with certain chemicals in the skin. This reaction produces substances that can absorb damaging rays from the sun. These light-absorbing substances prevent the rays from penetrating deep into the skin where they can cause a severe sunburn. Over time, the damage caused by overexposure to the sun can lead to skin cancer.

Materials

* scissors
* newspaper
* white construction paper
* stapler
* marking pen
* 3 resealable plastic bags
* 2 sunscreen products (one with an SPF rating twice that of the other)

The damaging rays from the sun are called ultraviolet radiation. This radiation exists in two forms, ultraviolet-A (UVA) and ultraviolet-B (UVB). Sunscreens offer protection mainly against UVB. UVB is more powerful than UVA in producing a sunburn. UVB is also a cause of several types of skin cancer. Sunscreens are rated for how much protection they provide against UVB. This rating is known as the sun protection factor, or SPF. The label on a sunscreen indicates its SPF rating.

The SPF indicates the amount of protection offered against skin reddening from UVB compared to the time it takes for the skin to redden without sunscreen protection. The amount of time it takes for a person to develop a sunburn without protection is known as the minimal erythemal dose, or MED. Assume that a person's MED is 10 minutes before his or her skin starts to turn pink. If this person applied a sunscreen with an SPF rating of 15, then he or she could stay in the sun for 15 times 10 minutes, or 150 minutes, before the skin turns the same color. A sunscreen with an SPF rating of 30 would allow the person to remain in the sun for 30 times 10 minutes, or 300 minutes. This is equivalent to five hours, or what is often a full day at the beach.

The degree of protection offered by sunscreens would seem to make it safe for a person to stay out in the sun all day without worrying about getting burned. However, sunscreens offer little, if any, protection against UVA. UVA is less likely than UVB to cause sunburn. But studies have indicated that UVA may be responsible for 90 percent of one type of skin cancer known as melanoma. Thus, sunscreens may prevent sunburns. But, over time, overexposure to the sun's rays can still lead to skin cancer, no matter how much sunscreen is applied.

This experiment will allow you to test whether a sunscreen with an SPF rating twice that of another sunscreen is really twice as effective in absorbing ultraviolet light. Rather than testing how quickly skin reddens, you will evaluate how quickly newspaper yellows because of exposure to ultraviolet light.

Cut three strips of newspaper and three equal-sized strips of white construction paper small enough to fit inside three resealable plastic bags. To keep the newspaper flat, staple the ends of each strip to a piece of construction paper. Place one sample in each of the three plastic bags and seal. Label the bags *A*, *B*, and *C*. Figure 14 shows how to make sure that the samples do not slide around whenever you move the plastic bags.

Apply a layer of one sunscreen to the outside of bag A, directly over the newspaper strip. Apply a layer of the other sunscreen to the outside of bag B, again directly over the newspaper strip. Bag C will have no sunscreen and serve as the control. Place the three bags in direct sunlight. Ultraviolet rays from the sun cause newspaper to turn yellow. Note how long it takes for each newspaper strip to start turning yellow. Obviously, the control should yellow first.

How does the sunscreen with twice the SPF rating stack up against the other sunscreen?

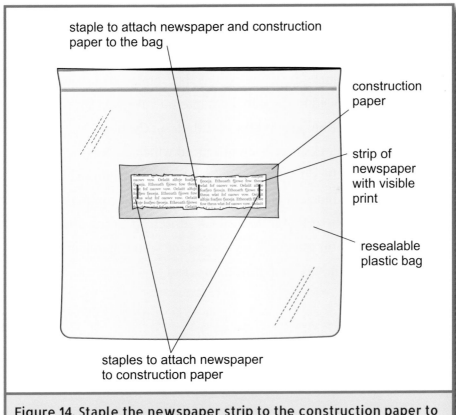

staple to attach newspaper and construction paper to the bag

construction paper

strip of newspaper with visible print

resealable plastic bag

staples to attach newspaper to construction paper

Figure 14. Staple the newspaper strip to the construction paper to keep it flat. Then staple the two through the bag to keep them in place.

You can expand this experiment to check out sunscreens with different SPF ratings. You can also compare expensive versus inexpensive brands with the same SPF ratings to see if the extra cost is justified. Of course, some sunscreens feel like rubber on your skin, while others let your skin breathe.

Project Idea

Sunblocks

Sunscreens absorb ultraviolet rays. Sunblocks actually deflect or turn away ultraviolet rays. Because they physically block the rays from penetrating the skin, sunblocks offer substantial protection against both UVA and UVB. But sunblocks do have one disadvantage. Sunscreens are absorbed by the skin and thus are invisible. In contrast, sunblocks are white creams that remain clearly visible after they are applied to the skin. Perhaps you have seen someone with a white "coating" around the mouth or on the nose.

Recently, sunblocks have been produced which are less conspicuous on the skin. As a result, people might be more likely to use such a sunblock in public. Design a project to compare the effectiveness of these sunblocks against sunscreens using photosensitive paper. You can check with someone who is familiar with photography for advice as to how to proceed.

Killing Bacteria

Another health care product that you might have at home is antibiotic cream. You may have applied an antibiotic cream to a cut on your skin. The cream is designed to kill any germs before they enter your body and cause an infection. This experiment will give you the chance to evaluate how well an antibiotic cream does its job.

Label the top of one large metal lid A, a second metal lid B. Prepare some plain gelatin according to the directions on the package. Be sure to add a tablespoon of sugar when dissolving the gelatin. The gelatin will serve as a surface on which bacteria can grow. The sugar will provide the nutrients for the bacteria. Before

Materials

* an adult
* 2 large metal lids
* marking pen
* plain gelatin
* tablespoon
* sugar
* 2 large metal lids like those from a mayonnaise jar
* plastic wrap
* refrigerator
* antibiotic cream
* cotton swab
* pair of rubber kitchen gloves
* pencil
* bleach

the gelatin hardens, pour a small amount into each of the two lids. Cover both lids with a piece of plastic wrap. Allow the gelatin to harden in a refrigerator overnight.

The next day, remove the plastic wrap and place a small dab of antibiotic cream on the gelatin in lid A. Use a cotton swab to spread the cream over the surface of the gelatin. Expose the gelatin in both

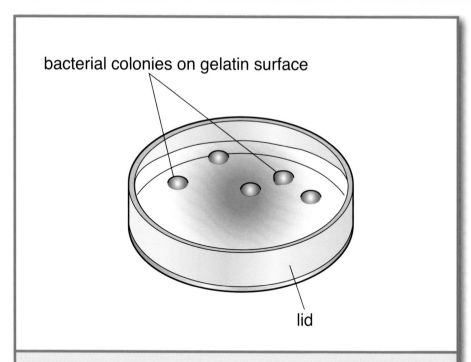

bacterial colonies on gelatin surface

lid

Figure 15. The colonies of bacteria that grow on the gelatin may have different shapes and color. Each represents a different type of bacteria.

lids to the air for 24 hours. Then seal each lid with plastic wrap. After several days, bacteria that landed on the gelatin will grow and multiply to form colonies, such as those shown in Figure 15.

Each type of bacteria can form a different-looking colony. Each colony represents millions of bacteria that developed from just one or a few bacteria that landed on that spot. Obviously, if the antibiotic cream was effective, then few or even no colonies should grow on lid A.

Bacteria that grow on the gelatin might cause some type of disease. To prevent coming in contact with any of these bacteria, do not touch the gelatin or lid. When you are finished making your observations, put on a pair of rubber kitchen gloves and finish your experiment **under adult supervision**. Use a pencil to poke a hole through the plastic wrap. Pour liquid bleach through the hole to cover the surface of the gelatin. Allow the lids to sit for 24 hours. The bleach will kill the bacteria. Carefully pour off the bleach, thoroughly rinse the lids under running water, and then dispose of them properly.

Chapter 4

MAKING YOU FEEL BETTER

Do you or someone you know take aspirin or pain relievers to cure a headache? Or perhaps you take an antacid tablet when your stomach feels queasy. A look inside the medicine cabinet in your home might show numerous medications that are used by someone in your family. These might include medications prescribed by a doctor to cure an infection, treat an eye irritation, or relieve the symptoms of an allergy. In addition to prescription medicines, you would also likely find a variety of over-the-counter medications. These can be bought without a prescription and might include pain relievers, stomach-acid neutralizers, and antibiotic creams.

By far, the most commonly used over-the-counter medication is aspirin. In fact, aspirin is the most widely used drug in the world. It is estimated that about one trillion aspirin tablets have been sold since it was first discovered one hundred years ago. In addition, more than 50 nonprescription drugs contain aspirin as the principal active ingredient.

Most medications are limited to the treatment of one specific problem or ailment. Aspirin, however, is used for a variety of medical problems. Aspirin reduces fever, pain, and the swelling of tissues caused by arthritis. It is also effective in preventing blood clots that can lead to a heart attack. Aspirin reduces the chances of a person developing a repeat episode of kidney stones. No other medication does so much. This is one reason why the aspirin industry has developed into a multibillion-dollar industry since it first began in the late 1800s.

The first recorded use of aspirin actually dates from the early Romans and Greeks. These people discovered that the bark, fruit, and leaves from certain shrubs and trees were helpful in treating pain and other problems. Native Americans later discovered that a liquid prepared from the bark of willow trees reduced fever and lessened pain. But these early users of aspirin had no idea about

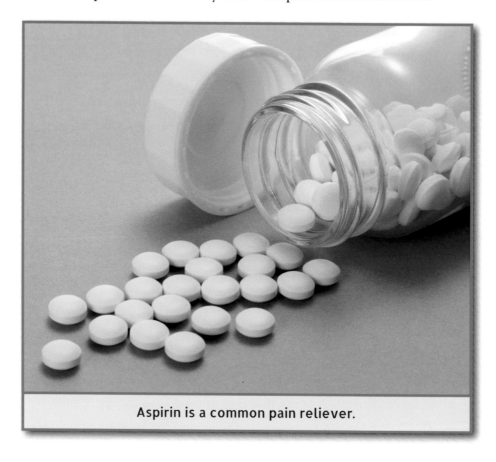

Aspirin is a common pain reliever.

the chemical nature of what they were taking. In the mid-1800s, scientists uncovered the active ingredient in these plants that could relieve pain and do so many other things. This ingredient has the chemical name salicylic acid. Once its chemical identity had been revealed, scientists could make pure salicylic acid in the laboratory.

But the cost of making salicylic acid was high. In addition, the chemical was found to be extremely irritating to the stomach. Then in 1897 a young scientist named Felix Hoffman discovered a way of changing this chemical into something less irritating but still as powerful. What Hoffman made is called acetylsalicylic acid. In 1899 the Bayer Company introduced this new pain reliever to the public under the name Aspirin. If you check the ingredient label on a bottle of any aspirin product today, you will see acetylsalicylic acid listed. This experiment will give you an opportunity to analyze an aspirin tablet and see what else it contains besides acetylsalicylic acid.

Manufacturers list how much acetylsalicylic acid is contained in each aspirin tablet. Check the label on a container of aspirin. Usually, a tablet contains 325 milligrams (mg) of acetylsalicylic acid. But an aspirin tablet contains more than just acetylsalicylic acid. To find out what percent of a tablet is actually acetylsalicylic acid, you must know the weight of a single tablet. Check the label for the weight of a single tablet. If it is not included on the label, weigh several tablets on a balance that measures grams.

Materials

* aspirin tablets
* metric balance
* wax paper
* large spoon or small hammer
* small glass jar
* measuring cup
* sugar test strip (available at a pharmacy)
* Lugol's solution

Once you know the measurement in grams (g), convert to mg by multiplying by 1,000. Divide the number of mg you get by the number of tablets you placed on the balance. This will give you the weight of a single tablet in mg. A single adult aspirin tablet should weigh about 500 mg. Calculate the percent of acetylsalicylic acid in each tablet by using the following equation:

$$\frac{\text{acetylsalicylic acid (mg)}}{\text{weight of tablet (mg)}} \times 100 = \text{percent of acetylsalicylic acid per tablet}$$

Manufacturers use fillers to give the tablet bulk and to prevent it from crumbling. Both sugars and starches may be used as fillers. To test if your aspirin contains these fillers, fold two tablets in a piece of wax paper. Use a large spoon or small hammer to crush the tablets. Transfer the crushed tablets to a small glass jar and add 1 fluid ounce of water. Aspirin does not dissolve in water, so be sure to swirl the jar gently to disperse the crushed tablet when carrying out the following steps.

Dip a sugar test strip in the liquid. Check the color of the strip against the chart on the container. Does your aspirin contain sugar as a filler? Next, add ten drops of Lugol's solution to the liquid. A royal blue color indicates the presence of starch. Does your aspirin contain starch as a filler? Finally, calculate the cost per tablet by dividing the price of the bottle of aspirin by the number of tablets in the container. Remember that the price per tablet decreases as the number of tablets per container increases. When comparing prices per tablet between brands, be sure the bottles contain the same number of tablets. You can repeat this experiment to evaluate different aspirin brands, including extra-strength products and ones intended for children. Based on your results, is there one aspirin product you would make a point to purchase in the future?

Project Idea

Buffers

The name *acetylsalicylic* acid tells you something about this chemical. It belongs to a group of chemicals known as acids. An acid can be defined in several ways. One way to classify a chemical as an acid is whether its water solution tastes sour. A more scientific way to classify a chemical as an acid is whether its water solution has a pH of less than 7. The pH of a solution indicates how acidic or basic a solution is and ranges from 0 to 14, as shown in Figure 16. A solution with a pH between 0 and 7 is an acid; one with a pH of 7 is neutral; and one with a pH between 7 and 14 is a base.

The pH of two aspirin tablets in a small glass of water is 2.7. This is about the same as the pH of apple juice. This level of acidity can be upsetting to the stomach of some people. To avoid any problem, these people are advised to drink a lot of water when taking aspirin. This dilutes the acidity of the aspirin. These people can also take buffered aspirin, which is made by combining acetylsalicylic acid with another ingredient. This combination produces a product that has a higher pH value than regular aspirin.

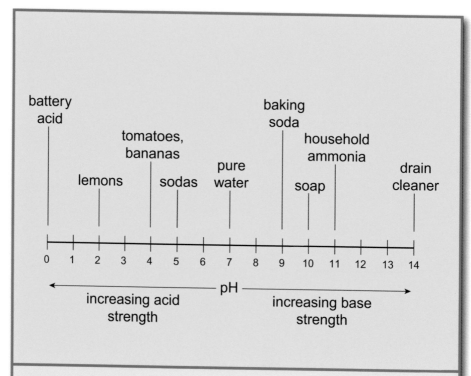

Figure 16. Which of the household items is the most acidic? Which is the most basic?

There are several ways to measure pH. You can use a pH meter or pH paper. Check with your science teacher to see if either a pH meter or pH paper is available. You can also measure pH with the help of an indicator. An indicator is a chemical that is used to determine the pH of a solution. Juice extracted from red cabbage is an excellent indicator. Experiment 4.3 describes how to extract and use the juice from red cabbage to measure pH. Use one of these methods to check buffered aspirin products to see how much less acidic they are than regular aspirin. Also analyze buffered aspirin as described in Experiment 4.1.

As part of your project, include information on how the buffer reduces stomach irritation. The mechanism involves changing acetylsalicylic acid into something called acetylsalicylate ions. The way buffers work is quite involved. If you decide to undertake this project, check with a chemistry teacher for guidance.

Analyzing Aspirin Substitutes

Some people are allergic to aspirin. These people should avoid taking aspirin because they can suffer serious side effects, including stomach bleeding. Those with ulcers must avoid aspirin because it could easily irritate their stomach lining. Children with the flu and a high fever must also not take aspirin because it can cause the children to develop Reye's syndrome. Reye's syndrome causes severe vomiting and can be fatal. To avoid the possibility of a child developing Reye's syndrome, some doctors recommend that aspirin should never be given to young children, even if they do not have the flu.

Materials

* aspirin substitute tablets (label must indicate amount of aspirin substitute per tablet)
* metric balance
* wax paper
* large spoon or small hammer
* 2 large drinking glasses
* measuring cup graduated in mL
* small spoon
* clock or watch
* 2 coffee filters
* funnel

To relieve pain and reduce fever, those who are advised to avoid aspirin must rely on aspirin substitutes. Various aspirin-free products are available. One product contains the chemical acetaminophen. Tylenol and Anacin-3 are brand names for products that contain acetaminophen. This chemical does not irritate the stomach or cause bleeding. However, acetaminophen can cause damage to the liver or kidneys if taken in high doses for several weeks.

Another aspirin substitute is ibuprofen. Advil and Motrin are brand names for products that contain ibuprofen. Like acetaminophen, ibuprofen does not cause Reye's syndrome. But ibuprofen, like aspirin, can irritate the stomach. This irritation can be avoided if ibuprofen is taken with food.

In this experiment, you can analyze an aspirin substitute product that you may have in the medicine cabinet at home. You can calculate the percent of active ingredient in a tablet using two different methods. One method was described in Experiment 4.1. The following experiment will introduce a second method and also involve percent error. Percent error is important to consider when reporting a measurement. Percent error indicates how different the results of an experiment are from the true or actual value. Scientists must consider percent error when reporting a measurement. Here is your chance to do the same. But before you do this, you must take a look at how measurements are made.

Up to this point, you have mainly used a nonmetric system of measurements. This system uses fluid ounces for volume and pounds or ounces for weight. The reason for having used this system is that most household measuring devices, such as cups and thermometers, are graduated in nonmetric units. The United States is one of the few countries in the world that does not use the metric system in daily activities.

The other system of measurements is the metric system. This system by most countries and by scientists throughout the world. You have used the metric system whenever you have measured volume in milliliters (mL) or weight in grams (g). The metric system is no more accurate than the nonmetric system. The only advantage is

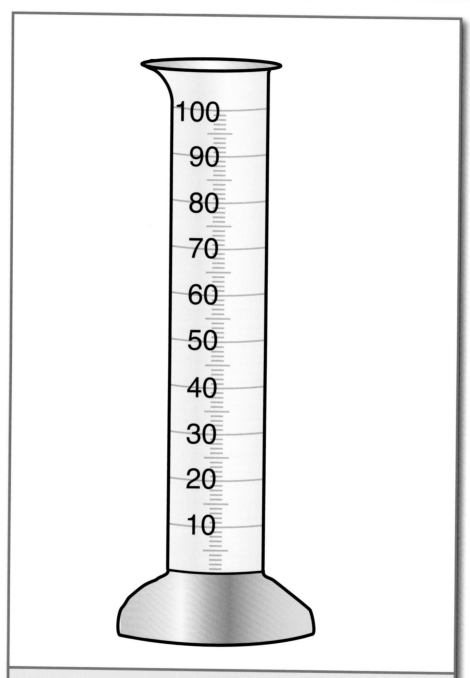

Figure 17. A graduated cylinder is the most commonly used piece of equipment for measuring volumes in a laboratory.

that the metric system is based on tens. This makes converting from one unit to another easy. For example, 0.325 g equals 325 mg (0.325 g x 1000 = 325 mg). All you have to do is move a decimal point when converting in the metric system. Compare this to converting 2½ pounds to ounces in the nonmetric system.

In this experiment, you will measure only in metric units. You will need a balance that records to tenths of a gram (0.1 g). Check with your science teacher to obtain such a balance. Inform your teacher that you need it to determine how accurate your measurements are. You will also need to measure volume in mL. You may have a measuring cup at home that is graduated in both nonmetric and metric units. If not, ask your science teacher if you may borrow a graduated cylinder like the one shown in Figure 17.

Place ten aspirin substitute tablets on a balance. Record their weight to the nearest tenth of a gram. Fold the tablets in a piece of wax paper. Use a large spoon or small hammer to crush the tablets into a fine powder. Transfer the powder to a large drinking glass. Add 200 mL of water to the powder. Both acetaminophen and ibuprofen dissolve in water. Use a small spoon to stir for five minutes to dissolve as much of the aspirin substitute as possible. Chemicals that are added as fillers do not dissolve in water. By determining how much of a tablet dissolves in water, you can calculate the percent of the aspirin substitute in a tablet.

Place two coffee filters on a balance. Record their weight to the nearest tenth of a gram. Fold one coffee filter and place it in a funnel. Place the funnel over another large drinking glass. Slowly pour the liquid containing the aspirin substitute powder through the filter, as shown in Figure 18. Swirl the liquid each time before you pour some into the filter. After all the liquid has passed through the

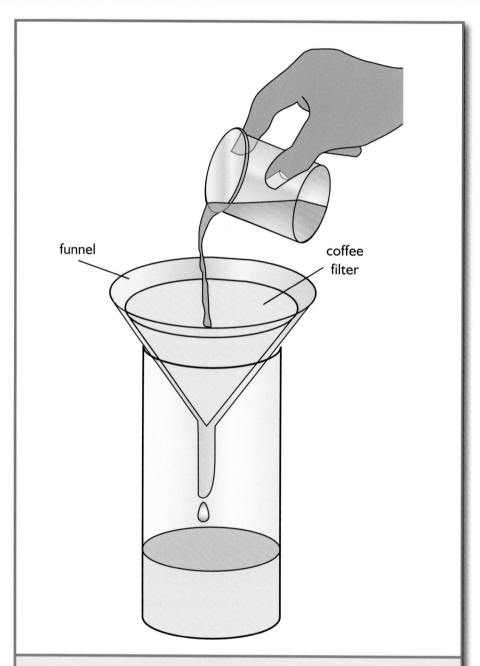

funnel

coffee
filter

Figure 18. Slowly pour the liquid into the coffee filter. Be sure that the level of liquid in the filter never gets higher than the top of the funnel.

filter, carefully remove the paper from the funnel. Place the filter somewhere where it can dry.

Filter the liquid that you collected in the glass once more. Do this by folding the second coffee filter as you did the first one and placing it in the funnel. Filtering the liquid a second time will trap any solids that may have passed through the first time. This time you can allow the liquid that passes through the filter to empty into a sink. After all the liquid has passed through the second filter, remove the filter and place it next to the first filter to dry.

When both filters are completely dry, weigh them. They should weigh more than before because of the solids they have trapped. Use the following formula to determine the percent of filler in your aspirin substitute tablet:

$$\frac{\text{weight of 2 filter papers and solids} - \text{weight of 2 filter papers}}{\text{weight of 10 aspirin substitute tablets}} \times 100 = \text{percent filler}$$

Subtract this value from 100 percent to calculate the percent of aspirin substitute in each tablet. This value represents your *measured value*.

Examine the label on the container of aspirin substitute you used. Note the amount of active ingredient in each tablet. This value is most likely recorded in mg. Multiply this value by 10 to determine the total amount of active ingredient in 10 tablets. Divide by 1,000, or move the decimal three places to the left, to change to g. Use the following formula to determine the percent of active ingredient in each tablet.

$$\frac{\text{total amount of aspirin substitute in 10 tablets (g)}}{\text{weight of 10 aspirin substitute tablets (g)}} \times 100 = \text{percent active ingredient}$$

This value represents the *true value*.

Use the following formula to determine the percent error in your experiment.

$$\frac{\text{true value} - \text{measured value}}{\text{true value}} \times 100 = \text{percent error}$$

When using this formula, do not be concerned if the difference between the true value and the measured value is a positive or negative value. Disregard the sign and just insert the difference between the two values in the formula.

Do not be concerned if your percent error seems large. There are many possible sources of error in this experiment. For example, some of the fillers used in the tablet may have dissolved in water. How would this affect your percent error? What are other possible sources of error? Can you refine your experiment to eliminate any of these sources?

One possible cause of an upset stomach may be too much stomach acid. To relieve an upset stomach, some people may take a commercial product that is designed to reduce excess stomach acid. Such products are known as antacids. An antacid is a weak base that can neutralize the excess acid secreted by a stomach. But is it possible for an antacid to neutralize all the excess acid? This experiment will provide the answer. You will extract the pigment from red cabbage to use as an indicator to determine if an antacid tablet has neutralized all the acid in a solution.

Tear the leaves of a red cabbage into small pieces. Place about one cup of torn leaves into a blender and cover with water. Blend the leaves until they have liquefied. If a blender is not available, place the cabbage pieces in a small pot, cover with water, and, **under adult supervision**, slowly boil until the water turns dark red. You may have to add some water to prevent the cabbage from burning. Filter

Materials

* red cabbage
* measuring cup
* blender, or small pot, stove, and an adult
* strainer
* 3 small glass jars
* lemon juice
* marking pen
* dropper
* distilled water (available at a pharmacy)
* antacid tablets
* wax paper (optional)
* large spoon or small hammer (optional)

the blended or boiled leaves through a strainer. Collect the filtered liquid in a clean glass jar. You will use this liquid as the indicator.

Pour 1 fluid ounce of lemon juice into a small glass jar. Label this jar *A*. Use a dropper to add the indicator from the red cabbage to the lemon juice. Be sure to add the indicator slowly until the lemon juice turns a distinct color. Observe the color that the indicator turns in lemon juice, which has a pH value of 2. This is the same value as the pH of the stomach's contents.

Pour 1 fluid ounce of distilled water into a second glass jar. Label this jar *B*. Add an antacid tablet to the distilled water. If the tablet is a chewable type, crush it before adding it to the water. Fold the tablet in a piece of wax paper and crush it with a large spoon or small hammer. Use a dropper to add the red cabbage indicator to the antacid solution. Notice the color the indicator turns in the antacid solution, which has a pH value of 8.

Add one antacid tablet to the glass jar labeled A. Again be sure to crush the tablets first if it is the chewable type. Allow the contents to stand for 15 minutes, but stir occasionally. Is the solution in jar A now the same color as the solution in jar B? If not, add more antacid tablets, one at a time. How many tablets must you add so that the solution in jar A is the same color as jar B? You can repeat this experiment with different brands of antacid tablets. Which brand uses the least number of tablets to turn the solution in jar A the same color as jar B? You can also test liquid antacids. Which brand takes the least volume to turn the solution in jar A the same color as jar B?

Project Idea

The FDA Way

The procedure outlined in Experiment 4.3 is not the one used by the Food and Drug Administration (FDA) to determine the effectiveness of an antacid. You will need the help of a chemistry teacher if you want to do this project.

The FDA procedure calls for dissolving one antacid tablet in 70 mL of distilled water. Next, 30 mL of 1N hydrochloric acid is added. The contents are allowed to stand for 15 minutes with occasional stirring.

The contents are then titrated with 0.5N sodium hydroxide solution. Either a pH meter or an indicator—bromothymol blue or congo red—is used. With a pH meter, the volume of sodium hydroxide added to bring the contents to a pH value of 3.5 is recorded. In the case of an indicator, the volume of sodium hydroxide added to bring about a definite color change is recorded. In either case, the amount of acid neutralized by the antacid is calculated in a unit called milliequivalents.

The milliequivalents of acid neutralized = 30 mL (the volume of acid used) x 1N (the concentration of the acid) minus x mL (the volume of sodium hydroxide added) x 0.5N (the concentration of the base). For example, if 50 mL of sodium hydroxide were added either to bring the pH value to 3.5 or to change the color of the indicator, then the milliequivalents of acid neutralized would be calculated as follows:

$(30) \times (1) - (50) \times (0.5) = 30 - 25 =$ 5 milliequivalents of acid neutralized by the antacid tablet

Use the FDA procedure to evaluate the effectiveness of different antacid products. The higher the value of milliequivalents, the

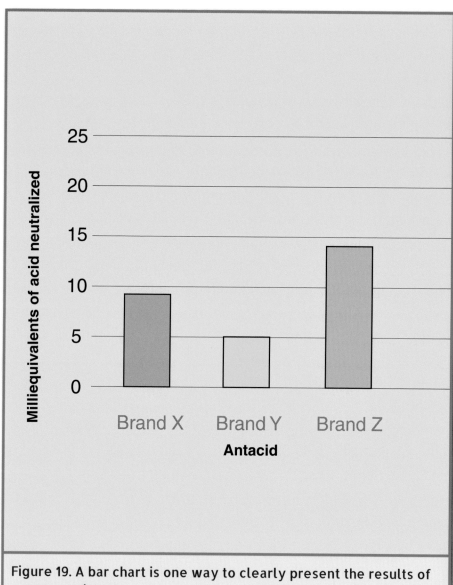

Figure 19. A bar chart is one way to clearly present the results of your experiment.

more effective the antacid. For example, a product that neutralizes 10 milliequivalents of acid is twice as effective as a product that neutralizes 5 milliequivalents of acid.

To test liquid antacids, the FDA calls for pouring the recommended dosage into a graduated cylinder. Distilled water is added to bring the volume to 70 mL. After adding 30 mL of 1N hydrochloric acid, the same procedure is followed that is used for antacid tablets. You can prepare a bar graph summarizing the findings of your project, such as the one shown in Figure 19.

Chapter 5

CLEANING HOUSE

Cleaning the house is not usually considered a fun way to spend time. However, many products have been invented and designed to make the job easier and more effective. In Experiment 1.1, you investigated how soap can dissolve grease. The soap you tested is a personal hygiene product designed for cleaning the body. Now we will take a look at cleaning products designed for household use—for cleaning dishes or washing clothes, for example. These cleaning products are not soaps, but rather detergents. Like soaps, detergents contain a chemical that allows water and grease to mix. This chemical is the key ingredient in any cleaning product and is called a surfactant. *Surfactant* is short for "surface-active agent". A surfactant is a chemical that allows water and grease to mix. A detergent may contain more than one kind of surfactant. Different detergents also use different types of surfactants.

Detergents also contain a variety of chemicals that perform different jobs. Some chemicals act as bleaches to eliminate stains. Others act as whiteners or as corrosion inhibitors to prevent rust from forming inside the washer. Still another chemical is added to detergent to eliminate a problem that can result from using soap: Chemicals in soap react with salts in water to produce a precipitate. A precipitate is a solid substance that does not dissolve easily in water. A familiar example of a precipitate that forms when soap reacts with salts in water is the ring left in a bathtub after bathing. This happens especially with water that contains a lot of salts and minerals. Water with a high salt and mineral content is known as hard water.

To prevent precipitates from forming, a chemical is added to detergent to soften the water. This water softener removes the salts and minerals present in water. The fewer salts and minerals present, the softer the water, and the less likely a precipitate will form. The chemical usually added to detergent as a water softener contains phosphate. Phosphates, however, pose an environmental problem. Phosphates are not biodegradable. This means that bacteria and other microorganisms cannot break down phosphates when they are released into the environment. As a result, phosphates can accumulate in bodies of water, such as lakes and ponds. There, the phosphates can serve as a food supply for algae, another type of microorganism. The algae can then use up all the oxygen in the water, suffocating fish and other organisms.

Because of their impact on the environment, detergents that contain phosphates have been banned by some communities and even by some states. However, many consumers have not been entirely happy with this ban because many phosphate-free detergents do not allow water and grease to mix very well. As a result, clothes may not get as clean as they would when washed with phosphate-containing detergents.

Experiment 5.1
COMPARING SOAP AND DETERGENT

In this experiment, you can evaluate how soaps and phosphate-containing detergents react in different types of water, ranging from pure water to hard water. Pure water, as its name implies, is 100 percent water containing practically nothing else. Sold as distilled water, this is considered extremely soft water.

Prepare some hard water by dissolving a tablespoon of Epsom salts in a cup of tap water. Place a piece of tape on each of six test tubes and number them 1 through 6. Half fill test tubes 1 and 2 with hard water, 3 and 4 with tap water, and 5 and 6 with distilled water. Add 10 drops of liquid hand soap to test tubes 1, 3, and 5. Add 10 drops of liquid dishwashing detergent to test tubes 2, 4, and 6. (See Figure 20a.)

Place your thumbs over test tubes 1 and 2. Shake vigorously for 30 seconds. Measure the height of the suds layer that forms in each test tube. Repeat this procedure with test tubes 3 and 4, and finally with test tubes 5 and 6. Which test tube(s) produced the most suds? Record your results in a chart like the one shown in Figure 20b. Try different brands of liquid detergent to see if one produces the most suds in hard water.

Materials

* tablespoon
* measuring cup
* Epsom salts (available at a pharmacy)
* tape
* 6 large test tubes
* marking pen
* distilled water (available at a pharmacy)
* dropper
* liquid hand soap
* liquid dishwashing detergent
* clock or watch
* ruler

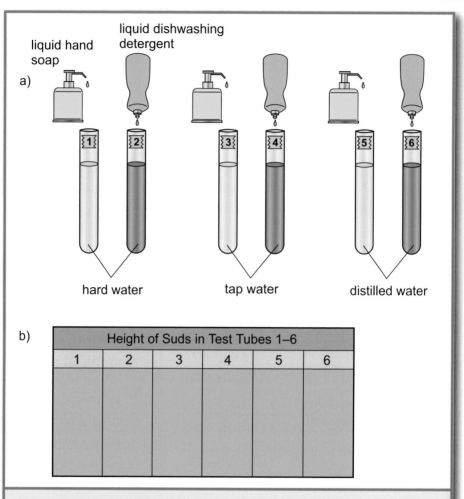

liquid hand soap

liquid dishwashing detergent

a)

hard water

tap water

distilled water

b)

Height of Suds in Test Tubes 1–6					
1	2	3	4	5	6

Figure 20. a) The experimental setup for Experiment 5.1 is shown. Add 10 drops of liquid hand soap to test tubes 1, 3, and 5 and 10 drops of liquid dishwashing detergent to test tubes 2, 4, and 6. b) Record your results in a chart.

The minerals in hard water bind up some of the soap, resulting in less suds being formed. In hard water, you have to add more soap to get the job done. Phosphate-containing detergents dissolve better in water, producing more suds. Because they dissolve better, you do not need to add more detergent to get the job done.

Experiment 5.2

CHECKING OUT AN EMULSIFIER

As with soap, the efficiency of a detergent is determined by its ability to emulsify grease that traps dirt. Emulsify means to mix water with grease or oil. You learned in Chapter 1 that oils and grease do not mix with water. Soaps and detergents are both examples of emulsifiers, which are substances that are used to mix two other substances that do not normally mix. Figure 21 shows how an emulsifier works. In this experiment, you can determine how well a detergent works as an emulsifier.

Materials

* test tube
* methylene blue (available as a pH indicator from a pet store)
* dropper
* plastic wrap
* clock or watch
* olive oil
* liquid dishwashing detergent

Add tap water to a test tube so that it is approximately a quarter full. Add three drops of methylene blue. Cover the test tube with plastic wrap and shake for five seconds. Remove the plastic wrap and add olive oil so that the test tube is half full. Two distinct layers will form. Which layer remains on the bottom? In which layer does the methylene blue dissolve?

Add ten drops of liquid dishwashing detergent. Cover the test tube with plastic wrap and shake for 15 seconds. Allow the two layers to separate. Observe if any of the dye is dissolved in the olive oil. Because the dye dissolves in water, the more the detergent

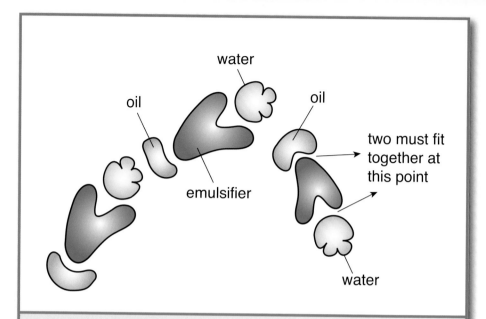

water

oil

oil

two must fit
together at
this point

emulsifier

water

Figure 21. An emulsifier can be used to mix two substances
that normally do not mix. One end of an emulsifier attracts one
substance, such as water. The other end of the emulsifier attracts
the other substance, such as oil, bringing the two substances
together.

emulsifies, the more dye will be present in the olive oil. You can
tell this by observing how dark the olive oil layer gets. Try different
brands of liquid detergent to see if one emulsifies best.

Blowing Big Bubbles

In Experiment 5.2, liquid dishwashing detergent was used to emulsify oil and water. But liquid detergents can also be used for something that is purely fun to do: making soap bubbles. If you have ever tried to blow bubbles with only water, you know that this does not work. You must add liquid soap or liquid detergent to the water. Only then can you make some interesting soap bubbles. A soap bubble is like a balloon. Bubbles and balloons both consist of a very thin skin that surrounds a volume of air. In the case of a bubble, the skin consists of a thin layer of soap and water, as you can see in Figure 22.

Soap is a chemical that consists of a long chain. One end of the chain is attracted to water. This end is shown as the small circles in Figure 22. The other end of the chain is attracted to grease or oil. This end is shown as the small tails in Figure 22. Notice that the tails attracted to the grease stick out from the surface of the bubble. Grease does not evaporate. As a result, a soap bubble can last for some time.

Materials

* measuring cup
* liquid dishwashing detergent
* liquid tincture of green soap (available at pharmacy)
* glycerin (available at pharmacy)
* 2 pie pans
* pliers
* several metal coat hangers
* piece of metal wire
* coffee stirrer
* an empty aquarium
* baking soda
* vinegar

If a soap bubble is placed in a closed container that is saturated with water vapor, the bubble can last even longer. Some people have blown bubbles that have survived for months and even almost up to year. Try your hand at making soap bubbles in this experiment.

You can use either a liquid dishwashing detergent or tincture of green liquid soap to make your own soap bubble liquid. To make your own soap bubble liquid, mix 4 cups of water, 12 teaspoons of glycerin, and 8 teaspoons of liquid tincture of green soap. You can get glycerin and green soap liquid from a pharmacy. Let the liquid stand for 24 hours before using it to blow bubbles. If you use a liquid dishwashing detergent, mix 8 cups of cold water with

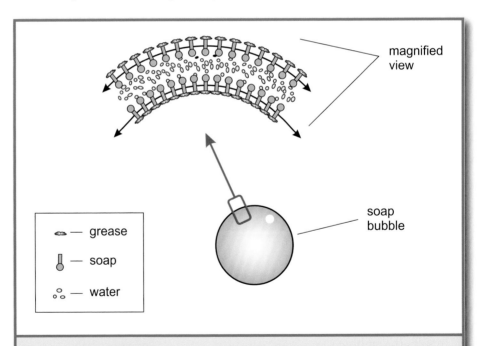

Figure 22. In a bubble, two layers of soap form a thin skin. Trapped between these two layers is water. One side of the soap molecule attracts water. The other side attracts grease or oil, forming a layer on both the outer and inner surfaces of the bubble.

the detergent. Add 1 tablespoon of glycerin. Let the liquid stand overnight.

Pour the soap solution into a pie pan. Use pliers to bend a metal coat hanger into the shape of a square, circle, or star. Be sure that the shape can fit into the pie pan. Gently place the hanger on the surface of the soap solution. Carefully lift the hanger and draw it through the air. What is the biggest bubble you can make? *The Guinness Book of World Records* lists the biggest soap bubble as spanning 156 feet with a surface area of approximately 4,000 square feet. Fan Yang created this monstrous "bubble wall" in 1997 to promote the 11th Annual Bubble Festival held at the Kingdome Pavilion in Seattle, Washington.

Bend a piece of metal wire into the shape of the wand that usually comes with soap bubble solution. Of course, you can use the real thing if you have such a soap wand. Dip the wand into the soap solution and blow a bubble. Use a coffee stirrer to blow a bubble inside a bubble. See how many bubbles you can blow inside another.

Place a pie pan in an empty aquarium tank and add half a cup of baking soda. Slowly pour a cup of vinegar into the pie pan. Observe what happens. The bubbles you see are carbon dioxide gas that forms when the baking soda and vinegar react. Gently blow a bubble so that it floats above the aquarium. Your bubble will sink into the carbon dioxide in the aquarium. Notice what happens to the bubble. The bubble gets larger because the carbon dioxide enters the bubble as it sinks.

Check the Internet for recipes on making soap bubble solutions. What kinds of soap bubbles can you make? You may also want to check out why soap bubbles produce such interesting colors.

It has to do with the way light waves behave. This behavior is called destructive interference and constructive interference.

Project Idea

Antibubbles

As its name suggests, an antibubble is the opposite of a bubble. A bubble is a thin film or skin of liquid that has air both inside and outside. In contrast, an antibubble is a thin film of air that has liquid both inside and outside. The difference between the two is illustrated in Figure 23. The liquid inside and outside an antibubble is usually water. If you blow air bubbles into a liquid, they will quickly rise to the surface. However, if you make antibubbles in a liquid, they take a long time to rise to the top. Not much has been written about antibubbles, but the Internet will have some Web sites to help get you started if you are interested in doing a project with antibubbles. Some Web sites explain how to make antibubbles, discuss their importance, describe some projects that you can undertake, and link you to other sites.

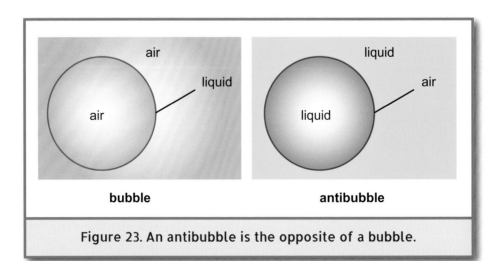

bubble

antibubble

Figure 23. An antibubble is the opposite of a bubble.

FLOATING ON WATER

Have you ever seen an insect walk on water? An insect is able to do this because of the surface tension of water. Surface tension causes a thin film of water to form on the surface. It is caused by the attraction that water molecules have for one another. A molecule is an individual particle of a certain substance, such as water. Chemists often use formulas when talking about molecules. You probably are familiar with the formula for a water molecule: H_2O.

Materials

* small bowl
* paper clips
* fork
* liquid dishwashing detergent
* measuring cup
* large spoon
* glycerin
* bubble wand

Picture a glass of water. Because of the way water is built, each H_2O molecule is attracted to two other H_2O molecules. In turn, each of these two H_2O molecules is attracted to two other H_2O molecules, and so on. This makes for a lot of attraction in a glass of water. All this attraction at the surface of the glass produces a thin film of water molecules upon which an insect can walk. In the following experiment, you will investigate how liquid detergent affects surface tension.

Fill a small bowl with water. Gently rub a paper clip across your forehead. This will transfer a little of the grease from your forehead to the paper clip. The grease will prevent water from sticking to the paper clip. Using a fork, lower the paper clip onto the water in the

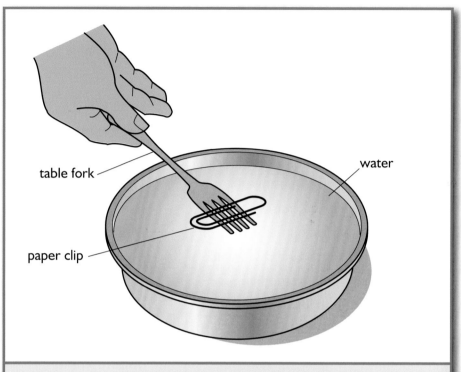

Figure 24. Use a fork to gently place a paper clip on the surface of the water.

bowl, as shown in Figure 24. Surface tension will support the paper clip. How many paper clips can you get to float on water?

Remove the paper clips from the water. Add 1 fluid ounce of liquid dishwashing detergent to the water. Use a large spoon to mix the detergent and water. Stir gently to avoid making suds. Now see how many paper clips you can get to float. Explain your observations. Check to see if liquid dishwashing detergents have the same effect as liquid laundry detergents. You can also test different brands.

In Experiment 5.3, glycerin was one of the ingredients needed to make soap bubbles. Glycerin makes the soap bubbles stronger and thus last longer. To find out why glycerin has this effect, investigate how the concentration of glycerin added to a detergent solution affects the surface tension of water. In this case, the concentration of the glycerin is the independent variable, while surface tension is the dependent variable. The concentration of the soap solution must be kept constant.

For each glycerin-detergent solution you prepare, use a bubble wand to blow a soap bubble. Determine if different solutions produce different-sized bubbles. If so, this will show that there is a relationship between the surface tension of a detergent solution and bubble size.

Experiment 5.5

GETTING OUT STAINS

Another cleaning product you probably have at home is liquid bleach. Bleaching involves a chemical reaction that removes the color from a substance. When used for washing clothes, bleaches preserve whiteness and remove stains. Care must be taken when using bleaches because they contain chemicals that can damage delicate fabrics such as silk. They can also damage sensitive skin. Repeated use of bleaches may cause cotton fabrics to turn yellow.

One way to avoid these problems is to use bleach that does not contain chlorine. In this experiment, you can compare bleaches with and without chlorine to see how well they remove

Materials

* an adult
* scissors
* piece of white cotton fabric
* crayon
* lipstick
* tomato juice
* 2 large glass jars of the same size
* marking pen
* liquid bleaches with and without chlorine
* clock or watch
* pair of rubber kitchen gloves

stains from fabrics. Conduct this experiment outside or in a place with good ventilation so that you do not inhale the fumes from the bleach.

Cut a piece of white cotton fabric into two equal-sized pieces. Stain both pieces with crayon, lipstick, and tomato juice. Try to make the stains—in terms of size and intensity of color—the same on both pieces of fabric. (Why is this important?)

Label one large glass jar as A and another as B. (Why must the jars be the same size?) Place a piece of stained fabric in each of the two jars. **Under adult supervision**, cover the fabric in jar A with bleach that contains chlorine. Cover the fabric in jar B with bleach lacking chlorine. Be sure that you add the same volume of bleach to each jar. What should be the only independent variable in this experiment?

Allow the fabrics to soak for 30 minutes. Put on a pair of rubber kitchen gloves and pour the bleach down a sink. Rinse the fabrics in running water for several minutes. Remove them from the jars and examine both fabrics. Was one bleach more effective in getting out stains? Will the less effective bleach work as well as the other if the fabric is allowed to soak in it for a longer time?

Project Idea

Bleaching Action

Everything is made up of very tiny particles called atoms. In turn, atoms are made up of even tinier particles. One of these is called an *electron*. An atom can lose one or more of its electrons. This is called an *oxidation reaction*. If an atom loses electrons, they must go somewhere. The electrons that one atom loses are gained by another atom. A *reduction reaction* involves the gain of one or more electrons by an atom. Thus, an oxidation reaction also involves a reduction reaction. Together, the two are referred to as a *redox reaction*.

Bleaches work by causing either an oxidation reaction or a reduction reaction. In both cases, the bleach works by changing a colored substance (stain) into a colorless substance. In other words, the substance that caused the stain is still in the fabric. But this substance can no longer be seen because the bleach caused it to become colorless.

Carry out a project that investigates how bleaches work in removing stains. You will first need to learn more about redox reactions. Ask a chemistry teacher for guidance. Compare the two types of bleaches in terms of their efficiency, rate of action, and how long they retain their bleaching ability. You can also investigate the optimum conditions in terms of water temperature and softness.

Experiment 5.6
CONDUCTING ELECTRICITY

Under the kitchen sink in your home may be a bottle of ammonia. If you have ever been nearby when a bottle of ammonia is opened, you know that it has a very sharp odor. This is the reason that ammonia is used to make smelling salts. In homes, ammonia is used as a cleanser, mainly to remove grease from stoves and kitchen countertops. Making ammonia for fertilizers is a major industry throughout the world.

Ammonia is actually a gas. But the ammonia in smelling salts, in bottles, and in fertilizers is not a gas. The ammonia in bottles is present as part of a substance called ammonium

Materials

* an adult
* insulated wire
* small lightbulb and socket (available at a hardware store)
* D battery
* scissors
* electrical tape
* small glass jar
* ammonia
* teaspoon
* sugar
* various household cleaning solutions

hydroxide. Ammonium hydroxide is made when ammonia gas reacts with water. The ammonia in smelling salts is present as ammonium carbonate. In fertilizer, ammonia is present as part of a substance called ammonium nitrate.

Ammonium hydroxide, ammonium carbonate, and ammonium nitrate can break apart in water. When they do, they form charged particles known as ions. An ion is a chemical substance that has either a positive charge or a negative charge. When ammonium hydroxide, ammonium carbonate, and ammonium nitrate break apart in water, they form both positive and negative ions. These ions can conduct electricity, as you can demonstrate in this experiment.

Connect a piece of insulated wire, a D battery, and a lightbulb as shown in Figure 25. Use electrical tape to hold the wire on the ends of the battery. If you did the wiring correctly, the bulb should glow. Electricity provided by the battery can flow through the circuit you have made to light the bulb. Use scissors to cut one of the wires leading from the battery. Now that the circuit has been broken, the bulb should no longer glow. Use the scissors to remove the insulation from both ends where the cut was made.

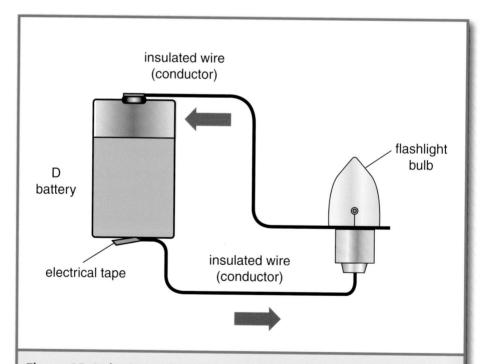

Figure 25. Strip the ends of the insulated wires with scissors. Use electrical tape to hold the bare ends against the battery. Hold the other ends against the bulb, as shown.

Under adult supervision, fill a small glass jar with ammonia. Place the bare ends of the cut wire into the ammonia. Observe what happens to the bulb. Obviously, ammonia restores the circuit that had been cut. Just as a wire can conduct electricity from the battery to light the bulb, so can the ammonia.

Two conditions must be met for a substance to conduct electricity. First, the substance must contain particles with both positive and negative charges. You read that ammonia in water meets this condition. Second, the charged particles must be able to move. The water in which the ammonia is dissolved allows the charged particles to move freely.

Pour the ammonia down a drain. Thoroughly rinse the glass jar with running water. Fill the jar with water and add one teaspoon of sugar. Stir until the sugar is completely dissolved. Check the sugar solution to see if it can conduct electricity. Obviously, one of the two conditions has been met. You have water, so if charged particles were present, they could move freely. Thus, what can you conclude does not happen when sugar dissolves in water? What other household cleaning solutions meet the two conditions required to conduct electricity? Find out by testing them to see if they allow electricity to flow, just as ammonia did. What would you conclude if one of the solutions causes the bulb to glow the brightest?

FURTHER READING

Churchill, E. Richard, Louis V. Loeschnig, and Muriel Mandell. *365 Simple Science Experiments With Everyday Materials.* New York: Black Dog & Leventhal Publishers, 2013.

Dutton, Judy. *Science Fair Season: Twelve Kids, a Robot Named Scorch, and What It Takes to Win.* New York: Hyperion Books, 2011.

Editors of TIME for Kids Magazine. *TIME For Kids Big Book of Science Experiments: A Step-by-Step Guide.* New York: TIME for Kids, 2011.

Henneberg, Susan. *Creating Science Fair Projects With Cool New Digital Tools.* New York: Rosen Publishing, 2014.

Margles, Samantha. *Mythbusters Science Fair Book.* New York: Scholastic, 2011.

Vickers, Tanya. *Teen Science Fair Sourcebook: Winning School Science Fairs and National Competitions.* Berkeley Heights, N.J.: Enslow Publishers, Inc., 2009.

WEB SITES

exploratorium.edu/snacks/index.html

Exploratorium Science Snacks *lists numerous activities that are miniature versions (snacks) of the most popular exhibits at the Exploratorium in San Francisco, California. Most of what you need to carry out these activities can be found at home.*

ipl.org/div/projectguide

The IPL's Science Fair Project Resource Guide will help guide you through your science fair project.

sciencebuddies.org/science-fair-projects/project_guide_index. shtml

Let Science Buddies give you extra ideas and tips for your science fair project.

SCIENCE SUPPLY COMPANIES

Arbor Scientific
P.O. Box 2750
Ann Arbor, MI 48106-2750
(800) 367-6695
arborsci.com

Carolina Biological Supply Co.
P.O. Box 6010
Burlington, NC 27216-6010
(800) 334-5551
carolina.com

Connecticut Valley Biological Supply Co., Inc.
82 Valley Road, Box 326
Southampton, MA 01073
(800) 628-7748
ctvalleybio.com

Delta Education
P.O. Box 3000
80 Northwest Blvd.
Nashua, NH 03061-3000
(800) 258-1302
delta-education.com

Edmund Scientifics
532 Main Street
Tonawanda, NY 14150-6711
(800) 818-4955
scientificsonline.com

Educational Innovations, Inc.
5 Francis J. Clarke Circle
Bethel, CT 06801
(203) 748-3224
teachersource.com

Fisher Science
300 Industry Drive
Pittsburgh, PA 15275
(800) 766-7000
new.fishersci.com

Nasco
P.O. Box 901
901 Janesville Avenue
Fort Atkinson, WI 53538-0901
(800) 558-9595
enasco.com

Sargent-Welch/VWR Scientific
P.O. Box 92912
Rochester, NY 14692-9012
(800) 727-4368
SargentWelch.com

Ward's Science
P.O. Box 92912
5100 West Henrietta Road
Rochester, NY 14692-9012
(800) 962-2660
wardsci.com

INDEX

57–58, 60–63, 68–70
vitamin solubility, 66–68
vitamin stability, 63
henna, 37
Hoffman, Felix, 81

I

ibuprofen, 87
insomnia, 41
ions, 115–117

L

Leeuwenhoek, Antoni van, 17
Lind, James, 57–58
Lugol's solution, 62

M

magnesium silicate hydroxide, 48
marjoram, 41
measured values, 91
medications
    antacids, 93–97
    aspirin, 79–83
    aspirin substitutes, 86–92
    buffers, 83–85
    fillers, 83, 91
    titration procedure, 95–97
melanoma, 72
Metric measurements, 87–89
microorganisms
    anti-bacterial soaps, 25–28
    history, 17–19
    liquid soap, 23–28
    shampoos, 32–35
    soap, 20–22
    toothpaste, 29–31
minimal erythemal dose (MED),
    72
Mohs, Friedrich, 48
Mohs hardness ratings, 48, 49

monomers, 51, 52
Motrin, 87

N

natural toothpastes, 31
nose cells, 39
nutrition. see health, nutrition
nylon, 52

O

oxidation-reduction reaction,
    113–114

P

pellagra, 58–59
percent error, 87, 92
pH, 83–85
phosphates, 100
planarians, 69–70
plaque, 29
polymers, 51–52
precipitates, 100
price comparisons, 83

Q

quartz, 49

R

records, documentation, 11–12
recycling, 54–55
Reye's syndrome, 86, 87

S

safety, 14–15
salicylic acid, 81
science fairs, 13–14
scientific method, 9–11
scurvy, 57–58, 60
sebum, 32
Semmelweis, Ignaz, 19

skin, 25
smelling salts, 115
sodium lauryl sulfate, 30
solid wastes, 54–55
solute, 66
solvent, 66
sun protection factor (SPF), 71–72
surfactants, 99

T

Takaki, Kanehiro, 58
talc, 48
tooth decay, 29
topaz, 49
triclosan, 27
true values, 91
turbulence patterns, 23–24
Tylenol, 86

U

ultraviolet radiation, 71–72

V

variables, 12–13
viscosity, 34
vitamin A, 69
vitamin B, 68–69
vitamin C (ascorbic acid), 57–58, 60–63, 68–70
vitamin K, 25, 66
vitamin overdosing, 68–70
vitamins, 59
vulcanized rubber, 52

W

water retention, 53–54
water softeners, 100